"*Taking Center Stage* is unlike any other book on public speaking. If you are about to take the limelight, this is the book to get you ready. I found the concept of treating a speech as an actor would a role to be thoroughly mind-changing. Everything else—poise, confidence, clarity, impact—flows perfectly from that premise."

—Sheryl J. Swed, president, U.S. Committee for UNIFEM
(United Nations Development Fund for Women)

"Even in our first coaching interactions with Deb and Buzz—years ago now—we were struck by the fundamental correctness of their approach, and by their powerful impact on our performance. And now it's all gathered together in a book! From the hard work of research and writing and rehearsal through to their advice on audience analysis, graphic exhibits, and strategy, I can't think of a more helpful guide to the corporate presenter than *Taking Center Stage*. They bring to their craft and their teaching what legions of communications consultants cannot—a proven, thoughtful methodology for approaching and mastering the art of public speaking."

—Derek van Bever, chief research officer,
The Corporate Executive Board

TAKING CENTER STAGE

Masterful

Public Speaking

Using

ACTING SKILLS

You Never

Knew You Had

DEB GOTTESMAN and **BUZZ MAURO**

BERKLEY BOOKS, NEW YORK

A Berkley Book
Published by The Berkley Publishing Group
A division of Penguin Putnam Inc.
375 Hudson Street
New York, New York 10014

This book is an original publication of The Berkley Publishing Group.

Copyright © 2001 by Deb Gottesman and Buzz Mauro
Text design by Tiffany Kukec

PRINTING HISTORY
Berkley trade paperback edition / June 2001

The Penguin Putnam Inc. World Wide Web site address is
www.penguinputnam.com

Library of Congress Cataloging-in-Publication Data

Gottesman, Deb.
    Taking center stage : masterful public speaking using acting skills you never knew
you had / Deb Gottesman and Buzz Mauro.
        p.   cm.
    Includes index.
    ISBN 0-425-17832-3
    1. Public speaking.   I. Mauro, Buzz.   II. Title.

PN4121 .G59 2001
808.5'1—dc21

2001025103

PRINTED IN THE UNITED STATES OF AMERICA

10 9 8 7 6 5 4 3 2 1

Contents

/

Acknowledgments

We'd like to thank the following people for their wisdom and support:

Julia Agostinelli, Amy Austin, Ginjer Buchanan, Lisa Considine, Laura Derrick, Colleen Estep, Michael and Roberta Gottesman, William H. Graham, Buzz and Marguerite Mauro, Michael Rodgers, and Lynn Seligman.

We would especially like to thank Steve Daigler and Jeanne Goldberg, without whom this book, and so much else, would not have been possible.

TAKING CENTER STAGE

Prologue

The Speaker As Actor

"When I speak of an orator, I speak almost as if I spoke of an actor."
—MARCUS TULLIUS CICERO, *perhaps the most famous speaker of all time*

BACK IN 1992, WE OPENED A SMALL ACTING STUDIO IN Washington, D.C., a town where lawyers and politicians outnumber theater artists by something like a thousand to one. Consequently, many of the students who walked through our doors came not out of a desire to be the next Marlon Brando or Meryl Streep but rather to develop skills that would help them stand out in a professional marketplace that puts a particularly high premium on spoken communication.

Several years later, acting training for non-actors had become more popular than we ever could have imagined. To help meet the demand, we created a consulting firm that deals exclusively with the application of acting techniques to the work of public speakers and other business professionals. Today our client list includes some of the most high-profile institutions in the public and private sector.

Actors were once considered society's most marginal citizens—

generally regarded as fools; periodically institutionalized as mad-men; and until the eighteenth century, forbidden the sacraments of the church in parts of Italy and Spain unless they forswore their vile profession. But times have changed. Suddenly actors have become the people to turn to when it comes to unlocking the secrets of high-powered public speaking. And it's about time, really, because— as Cicero pointed out civilizations ago—the successful orator is, in almost every conceivable way, simply an actor by another name.

Actors know how to make a lasting impression. They know how to speak naturally and powerfully, even when they're saying some-one else's words. They know how to project personality. They know how to harness the power of the imagination. They know how to analyze a role and play it to the hilt. They know how to stay cool with hundreds of people staring at them. They have at their disposal vocal and physical techniques to maximize the effectiveness of their communication. They specialize in connecting with an audience. And, perhaps most important, they know that self-confidence and powerful communication skills come from practice, and they know what kind of practice is most valuable.

No matter what kind of speaking you plan to do—from a toast at a reception to a business presentation in a conference room to a televised speech for an audience of millions—the skills of the acting profession will make you the best public speaker you can be. When you finish this book, you'll have mastered the techniques necessary to take the stage with confidence and enthusiasm, deliver a com-pelling message, and offer your audience a meaningful experience that they'll remember long after the applause has faded.

Chapter 1

An Actor Prepares

"Surely we have always acted; it is an instinct inherent in all of us."

—SIR LAURENCE OLIVIER

THE TALENT MYTH

Most people assume that good actors—and good public speakers—are good because they possess something called "talent." It's a word you hear a lot. Performers are "talented," or "gifted," meaning: They must have been born with it. But so far biologists have not isolated a talent gene, and it's pretty certain they never will. Talent is a figment of our collective imagination.

Maybe our culture has created this talent specter because we like to put valuable people on a pedestal. Maybe because effective performers sometimes seem to be endowed with powers that are not of this earth. Or maybe because it's just easier to say "I have no talent" than it is to work hard at developing a skill.

Of course, some people have to work less at public speaking than others to do it effectively. Maybe you're even one of them; if so, by all means use the T word. But the crucial point is: *Everyone can learn the skills required to captivate an audience.* It's not magic. You can *become* talented. All it requires is a willingness to look at things in new ways, to work hard, and to put yourself on the line a little bit. If you *dare,* you can do it, and do it well.

And we can go further: It's even possible to learn how to dare.

That's the foundation of this book. We wouldn't have written it if we didn't think it was possible to make you a better speaker.

Note that you are already a speaker, by the way, no matter what your level of podium experience. You do it all day long, unless you're a hermit. And graduating to "public" speaking from the more private variety is not as big a step as it may seem.

The best public speaking is very similar to the best everyday speaking. It is specific to the listener or listeners, it happens for a good reason, and it comes from the heart. It's basically just a form of conversation in which one or more of the conversationalists are not talking, or not talking very much. The conversation may be pumped up to reach a larger audience or to make a more important point than in most day-to-day talk, it may be more thoroughly prepared and strategized, but the most important aspect is identical: Whenever you talk, you talk out of a need to *make something happen.* You might be trying to solve a problem or secure a loan or get a date. Actors call it "pursuing an objective."

Plays are all about characters acting on each other to get what they want, be it love, money, or revenge. In the public speaking arena, the people you are acting on are, of course, the audience members—they make up the other characters in your "play." Your objective might be as simple as getting them to laugh at the groom on his wedding day or as complex as reversing their stand on abortion, but there's always something that you want from them, whether you realize it or not. By learning to approach your speech the way an actor approaches a script, you'll put the focus of your communication where "talented" speakers know it needs to be: on consciously affecting your listeners.

GETTING TO CARNEGIE HALL

Whatever your specific public speaking goals, it's important to realize that simply reading this book (or any other book) will not get you very far. You're going to have to practice. There's no other way to get good at it.

Public speaking, like all other forms of acting, is a physical activity. You do it with your body, just like playing tennis or the piano. You wouldn't make much progress if you never picked up a racquet or practiced your scales.

No actor in his right mind would take the stage without weeks of practice under his belt. What seems effortless to the audience is, in actuality, the result of carefully planned decision-making borne of hours of trial and error. The more you rehearse, the more confidence you have in the decisions you've made. It's as simple as that.

Take a look at the rehearsal habits of contemporary actors, and you'll nearly always find a direct correlation between those who embrace the rehearsal process and those we identify as truly "inspired" performers. Paul Newman and Al Pacino have both confessed to enjoying rehearsal even more than performance, wishing the experimentation phase of the artistic process could go on indefinitely. For Charles Durning, it does. Even after weeks of rehearsal, when his lines are fully committed to memory, he likes to read his play from cover to cover before each show, mining the text for new meanings. Or consider Madeleine Kahn: Praised throughout her life for her "natural" comic ability, she, in fact, relied on an extremely methodical preparation process. From the moment she accepted a role, she said, "It's in my brain and my computer is working on it. And it's an ongoing process until after the reviews are out."

While practice may never make us perfect, great actors know that it's the only reliable route to successful performance.

Yet amazingly, many public speakers don't practice. What little preparation they do consists of looking over their notes a couple of times before the big day, which means they often reach the moment of performance without having spoken the speech aloud a single time. Now, it should come as no surprise that underprepared speakers are more likely to ramble, mumble, sound stilted, lose their train of thought, and succumb to the worst of their unexamined habits, like shuffling their feet or filling their language with "ummms" and "aaahs." And they're generally more nervous, because they have a lot more to be nervous about. So why don't speakers prepare more?

In part, it's because rehearsal itself can be scary, so people avoid it. Practicing your speech reminds you that you'll soon be giving it, a reality that many anxious speakers would just as soon not face. Consequently, some people never force themselves to get up and do the speech full-out except when there's an audience present and the stakes are as high as they get. If you think of each of these performances as a rehearsal for future performances, the unprepared speaker is actually *rehearsing being nervous,* making the nervousness an integral part of the speaking experience in a horrible vicious circle.

How much better, then, to get up on your feet under controlled conditions, and give yourself a chance to *rehearse being in control.* A well-structured rehearsal process will promote the development of good performance habits that will serve you, even subconsciously, when you actually get around to delivering your presentation. Just as bad experiences will reinforce negative emotions, good ones will foster positive feelings about the speaking process. Great minds from Aristotle to William James have noted that the best route to becoming brave is simply acting brave. Likewise, the best route to becoming a good speaker is acting like one, which means rehearsing.

As you'll see, good rehearsals involve growth and exploration, always moving forward toward greater mastery of the presentation, never standing still. Far from forcing your presentation into a rigid form, a good rehearsal process gives you exciting new ways of looking at your material, your audience, and yourself.

Because a big part of any presentation is *self*-presentation, a big part of rehearsing is picking and choosing which parts of yourself you want to make use of. Good actors—the ones who always command your attention and are believable in widely different roles—are experts at accessing aspects of their *nonhabitual* selves. They know themselves well enough to be able to call up parts of who they are that they don't normally show to people, maybe even to themselves.

To be a commanding speaker, you'll need to do something similar. For example, you'll probably want to access those parts of yourself that are most confident, engaging, and persuasive. You don't want to hide your personality under a bushel, because it's your greatest asset, but you also don't want to define your personality quite as narrowly as you might be tempted to. A great acting teacher once said that every human being possesses all eighty-eight keys on the piano, but most of us restrict our melodies to the middle octave. The good news is, with the right kind of rehearsal everyone can become a virtuoso.

Some people might see a contradiction in this whole notion. Isn't acting essentially about faking? Doesn't sincerity play any role in public speaking?

The contradiction disappears when you begin to understand the true nature of acting. There's nothing phony about it. It's not about cheap "theatrics" designed to steal the show. Any person who gets onstage thinking like that may be a performer, but he's not an actor, at least not a good one. A real actor finds the *truth* in the character, the situation, the relationships, and the language. He brings many different aspects of himself to the role and lives it as honestly as he can, within the fictional parameters of the play. A good speaker does the same within the parameters of the speech.

The role of the public speaker is exactly that—a role. But it's no more fake than any of the other roles we play every day: neighbor, boss, employee, parent, sibling, friend. You're different in every role—you don't behave the same way with your mother as you do with your daughter—but each one is completely real. As a public speaker you may play the role of teacher, motivator, expert problem solver, jester, doomsayer. The techniques of acting will help you play them sincerely and effectively.

Of course, a certain amount of art is involved. You will not simply be presenting the whole truth and nothing but the truth. You will need to be natural, yet exciting. Logical, yet interesting. Personable, yet audible. To be a good actor you must aim not just for reality, but for a heightened reality. As you work through this book, our hope is that you'll come to understand what Oscar Wilde meant when he said, "I love acting. It is so much more real than life."

HOW TO USE THIS BOOK

How you work with this book depends on the type of speech you're giving and your level of preparation up to this point. If you've got a speaking engagement scheduled and you've not yet begun to prepare, the best way to use this book will be to start at the beginning and work your way through the whole thing. You'll receive step-by-step guidance in all aspects of speech development and performance, from putting pen to paper for the first time through graciously accepting your applause. The method presented here is a carefully structured, proven system, and if you do it all, it will have you speaking confidently and powerfully in the shortest possible time.

If, however, you're planning to deliver a speech you've already written or one that's been written by someone else, feel free to skim the writing sections. But don't skip them completely, because they can spark ideas for how to revise or interpret your text for structural consistency, internal logic, clarity and vividness, dramatic build, and appropriateness to your own speaking style.

It's certainly possible that your speech will not be written out at all. If you're speaking from notes, from memory, or entirely off the cuff, breeze through the sections about getting the speech on paper and interpreting the text, and focus more fully on the chapters dealing with affecting your audience and developing the skills of centered communication.

Of course, you may not even have a speech on the horizon. If you're reading this book to improve your public speaking skills but you're not currently preparing for a presentation, you can still practice the exercises. Just mock up a dummy speech on some topic that interests you, or find a book of famous speeches and use one of them. The skills you'll learn will readily transfer when it's time to do one of your own.

Chapter 2

Theatrically Speaking

"It is a simple fact that all of us use the techniques of acting to achieve whatever ends we seek, whether it is a child pouting for ice cream or a bawling politician bent on stirring the hearts and pocketbooks of potential constituents."

—MARLON BRANDO

SPEAKING WITH PURPOSE

Pretend for a moment that you're an actor in a play. You look at your script on the first day of rehearsal and see that you have this line: "Stella, Stella!"

How are you going to say it? Should it be loud or soft? Fast or slow? Do you think the first Stella should sound the same as the second, or somehow different? Should you act like you're in pain? Or should you just try to imitate Marlon Brando in the movie?

Well, who knows? There are a million ways to say the line, of course, and you could drive yourself crazy trying to choose among all the possible variations. That's why actors with some experience under their belts approach the issue in a very different way.

Instead of concentrating on *how* to say it, the experienced actor asks, "*Why* am I going to say this line?" And if he's a good actor, he'll then say to himself: "Because my character wants something, and saying this line will help him get it." His experience has shown him that this is true for every line of every play. Of course, there's more to it than that. He still has to figure out what it is that this particular character wants at this particular moment and why saying that line might get it for him, but he's on his way to a fruitful answer, one that will ultimately solve the problem of how the line gets said.

This actor knows that a good product is the result of a good process. The product he's after may be a riveting, ground-breaking, award-winning performance, but he starts with the basic process of figuring out what his character is trying to achieve by saying the lines in the script.

An actor playing Stanley Kowalski in *A Streetcar Named Desire* will, in fact, have the line "Stella, Stella!" If he's a good actor, rather than worrying about how to say it or what the reviewers will write about his delivery, he'll concentrate on the true purpose of Stanley's communication: to persuade his wife to take him back. What makes this a theatrically potent moment is Stanley's need to move Stella to action with his words.

This is the first principle that acting students learn: Actors *act*. They *do* things to affect the other characters in the play.

This is also the first principle of effective public speaking: The speaker must act on the audience. Specifically, he must persuade his audience to think, feel, or do something as a result of hearing him.

METHOD SPEAKING

All communication is intended to persuade. Whenever you talk, you're trying to affect someone, to get a response. If you say, "Get me a glass of water," you're probably trying to persuade someone to get you a glass of water. If you say, "Johnny got a C-plus on his arithmetic test," you may be trying to persuade someone to feel sorry for Johnny, or congratulate him, or spend more time with him in the afternoon.

Whenever we speak "in real life," it's out of *need*. We need a glass of water or we need to make Johnny feel better. We first experience the need, then we find something to say that will help us fulfill it. Most of us are very good at it. In fact, the process usually happens completely unconsciously.

Public speaking, on the other hand, often happens in reverse. By the time we actually start speaking behind a podium, the original impetus for the speech may be hard to connect to, or even to remember. We look at words on a page or on note cards—even if we wrote them ourselves—and see only words or, at best, intellectual ideas. The need is hidden. And if we go ahead and speak without activating the *need* to speak, the communication will be inauthentic. We'll probably appear unnatural and certainly will not be very effective.

To fulfill the persuasive function of a presentation, the speaker must first identify the need lurking beneath the text and then use the words to try to satisfy it. That calls for a reliable method of making fundamental communication into a conscious process—one that we can control.

Here's where a little acting training comes in handy. Actors are used to taking words that have already been written ("Stella, Stella!") and investing them with new life and urgency. That is, they know how to activate a need. This is the basis of Method Acting, a system that originated with Russian acting teacher Konstantin Stanislavsky around the turn of the last century. Because "the Method" has been espoused by such formidable actors as Marlon Brando, Dustin Hoffman, and Geraldine Page, some people mistakenly assume it's very mysterious or altogether abstruse. For others, the term conjures up silly extremes of "losing yourself in the role." The truth is that the basic principles of Method Acting are mostly just common sense, and they turn out to have great implications for public speakers.

Here's Method theory in a nutshell: In each moment of a play, every character has something that he wants or needs from another character or characters. These wants and needs are known as "objectives." Objectives can be short term (*I want this person to give me a hug*) or long term (*I want to earn this person's respect*). The means by which objectives are achieved are called "actions." Actions are the tactics a character uses to get what he wants from another character. A character's action might be to reassure, to amuse, to seduce, or to plead. Any strong verb will do. The Method actor's job is to consciously and specifically identify his character's objectives and then to take whatever actions are necessary to achieve them.

The rest of this chapter will look more closely at how the tools of actions and objectives apply to public speaking. In the next chapter you'll put these powerful concepts to work in your own speech.

The Audience As Scene Partner

A big part of the attraction of a play is that the audience gets to peek in on characters who don't know that they're being peeked in on. It's a voyeuristic thrill. But if you give a speech and appear not to know that the audience is there with you, they're sure to feel alienated, to say the least.

That means your audience is fundamentally different from the audience at a play. Your audience is essentially on the stage with you, an integral part of your scene. You're not creating something *for* them; you're creating something *with* them.

The actors in a play are concentrating on their scene partners, playing actions in pursuit of objectives that can only be satisfied by those other characters. (Stella is the only one who can take Stanley back.) In your presentation, your scene partner is the audience. They are the people you are acting on and only they can satisfy your objectives.

Defining Objectives

So what might your objectives be? What might you want from your audience?

The number one objective cited by inexperienced speakers is "to give them information." But if this is what tops your list, you're headed for trouble. "Giving information" may be a great way to generate yawns, daydreams, and excellent doodles from your audience; but if you want to create excitement or elicit change, you've got to go for something stronger.

Contrary to popular belief, presentations and speeches are not about stating facts. (If they were, you could just hand out a report and go home!) As the speaker, it's your job to exert influence. The audience is an active participant in the exchange because you, either implicitly or explicitly, ask them to agree with you or to make an important decision based on the arguments you are presenting.

One of your goals as a speaker, therefore, must be to get your audience *involved*. The only way to do that is to know from the start exactly what kind of involvement you're hoping for. That means your objective must require an active response from your listeners.

The formula for creating powerful speeches with strong, clear objectives is actually quite simple. Just fill in the blanks: "I'm telling you x so that you will do y." Most people have no problem identifying the x (after all, this is the subject matter of the speech—the information). It's the y variable—the objective—that sometimes proves tricky. Once you know y, you're ready to successfully address your public.

Let's say you're giving a talk about sexually transmitted diseases, or the history of your neighborhood, or this year's company P&Ls. Instead of simply imparting the information (*x*) to your audience:

- Educate them about STDs *so that they will abandon unsafe sexual practices.*

- Give a historical overview of your neighborhood *so that they will sign a petition to preserve historic homes.*

- Chart your company's decline in profits *so that they will not ask for a raise this year.*

As you can see, good objectives require that the speaker have a strong point of view. Everything you say must be designed to get your audience to see it your way and do what you want them to do. If you want to be persuasive, confident, entertaining, interesting, and an all-around great speaker, you start by knowing exactly what you want your speech to accomplish.

Choosing Objectives

It's important to note that your speech topic does not necessarily define or even limit your objectives. *What* you are talking about is very different from *why* you are talking about it. For instance, a speech to major investors about the volatility of the current stock market might suggest the following—highly dissimilar—objectives: (1) to make the investors pull out of companies lacking a proven track record, (2) to encourage investors to engage in rapid trading because the market is hot, or (3) to discourage investors from engaging in rapid trading because the market is about to cool. It all depends on your point of view about the topic and your relationship with the audience. You get to decide.

While some speeches might have only one objective (for example, a thirty-second commercial to get you to vote for a particular candidate) others may have a number of smaller objectives that serve a larger purpose. This larger purpose—the ultimate aim of the communication—is known in acting terms as the *superobjective*.

Here's an example of the relationship between objectives and superobjectives. In an hour-long stump speech, a long-shot candidate for governor might aim to accomplish the following:

- Persuade you that four more years under the current leadership will bankrupt your state.

- Get you to admit that your current school system is inadequate.

- Make you believe that tax increases are in everyone's best interest.

- Make you see the candidate as a leader.

Each of these objectives serves an obvious superobjective: *to win your vote*.

Playing Actions

But how are you going to *achieve* all these highly specific objectives? That's where actions come into the picture.

Inspire, enrage, illuminate, surprise, cajole, grab, exhilarate. These are all strong actions you can perform on the audience and excellent answers to the question, "What can I do to get what I want?"

The tactics by which you make your listeners see things your way and do what you want them to do should grow directly out of your objectives. Want the crowd to see you as a leader? *Inspire* them with a story about the time you stood up to City Hall. Want to earn their trust? *Disarm* them with a self-deprecating joke about a mistake you made and the lesson you learned. Want them to accept the need for a tax raise? *Alarm* them with bleak projections about depleted county services in the year 2010. Or *exhilarate* them with stories of wonderful new projects that could be created if each person gave just a little more. The possibilities are endless. But the actions you choose to perform should be specific to each moment and meaningful to the particular audience you are addressing.

There are many kinds of actions, and great speakers know how to exploit them all. Some actions are physical, like moving away from the podium to get closer to the crowd, softening a harsh line with a smile, or raising a fist in triumph. In chapter 6 we'll deal with physical actions in greater depth. Most actions you'll perform in the speaking situation, however, will be psychological: amusing the audience with ironic observations, arming them with cogent data, warning them about hidden costs, and so on. Even the psychological actions can be broken down into two basic types: those that appeal to emotion ("amusing them" falls into this category) and those that appeal to logic (for example, "making an argument based on statistical data"). Since different people respond to different approaches, most good speeches use a lively combination of the logical and the emotional.

You may have noticed that all the actions we've described so far are about *doing* something rather than *being* something. The difference is subtle but important. To *do* something is to act on your audience. To *be* something is to try to maintain an image. Think of the difference between "making the audience laugh" (a strong action, the success of which is easy to measure) and "being humorous" (a weak action because it implies no concrete result). Doing something is other-oriented; being something is self-involved. Although the being versus doing debate has raged on for centuries in the acting profession, contemporary thespians pretty much agree that "To be or not to be" is no longer the question. "To do and how to do" is what it's all about.

The Spice of Life

Students of public speaking talk a lot about finding variety in a speech. They are terribly afraid of being boring, so they make sure their speeches have soft parts and loud parts, smiley parts and frowny parts, and they never, ever stand in one place for too long. If you ask them why they decided to raise their voice in a particular moment or lean over the lectern, you're likely to hear, "I felt it was time for a change." Which is the same as: "No good reason."

There is no benefit to seeking variety for variety's sake. Your audience doesn't want to see you perform a bunch of random actions just to break up the monotony. In fact, physical or psychological changes that don't support the moment-to-moment objectives of the speech are likely to distract your listeners, or even confuse them. If you've ever heard a speaker who varied his pitch on every word or his tempo on every sentence, you know what we're talking about here.

The way you achieve good, meaningful variety in a speech is by knowing what you want to accomplish with each passage and developing a series of tactics or actions that will make those things happen. The best speeches change tactics often, affecting the audience with arguments and examples, stories and visuals, numerical data and emotional appeals. If you want to keep your presentation lively, do it by finding lots of ways to get through to your listeners.

Some of your tactics can be chosen beforehand, in the development stages of your speech, which you'll begin in the next chapter. For instance, if you know you want to decrease the emotional distance between you and your listeners, you can decide in advance to tell a story about how you grew up in a rural community just like theirs. If you want to get them to change their minds about animal slaughter, you can plan to bring an adorable baby calf on stage with you.

But there are some actions that you will discover only when you are in front of live human beings. That's because all good speaking, just like all good acting, is ultimately about *inter*action. The success of your communication depends not only on how you're performing your actions but also on how the audience is receiving them. That's why excellent speakers come to the moment of performance with specific, achievable objectives and strong ideas about actions that will help them achieve those objectives, they remain flexible enough to adjust their tactics if they need to.

In later chapters, you'll develop a rehearsal process that will help you know how it's playing in Peoria, so you can adjust your communication if necessary. For now, it's enough to keep in mind that everything you do on stage is intended to affect the audience in a particular way. The more specific your objectives and actions, the greater your chances of influencing your listeners.

Chapter 3

The Speaker As Playwright

*"The writer should, as much as possible, be an actor;
for they are the most persuasive and affecting who
are under the influence of actual passion."*

—ARISTOTLE, *Poetics*

IN THE BEGINNING, ACTOR AND DRAMATIST WERE ONE.
When Thespis took the prize in history's first recorded drama festival (Athens, 534 B.C.E.), his victory was all the more complete because he had written every word of his winning entry and performed every role. Over the years, of course, theater grew into a collaborative art, and the professions of playwright and actor diverged. But from William Shakespeare to Whoopi Goldberg, the tradition of the writer/actor has survived, in part because there will always be great artists who want to seize control of the expressive process at its origin.

In a performance as personal as a speech, that much control is a gift. It's certainly possible to do a great job with a speech that was written by someone else (presidents do it all the time), and the rehearsal techniques presented later in this book will give you many tools for doing that. But if you're developing your own presentation, you, like Thespis before you, have a great opportunity to maximize its dramatic potential before you even utter a word.

REINVENTING THE SPEECH PROCESS

If you had an eighth-grade English teacher who forced her students to learn something about public speaking, you probably encountered this traditional process for constructing a speech:

1. Choose a thesis.

2. Organize your main points.

3. Devise arguments to support your thesis.

This method will result in a well-organized speech, but it has several drawbacks. The most glaring is that it is entirely concerned with the speaker and does not even consider the role of the audience. It also places the emphasis on static information and ideas rather than dynamic objectives and actions.

For those reasons, we propose the following reinvention of the process:

1. Decide what you want your audience to do.

2. Assemble the information they must have in order to do it.

3. Interpret the information in such a way that they are persuaded to do it.

As you can see, this process puts the audience's needs at the center of the speech, where they belong, and uses what we know about the benefits of defining clear objectives and playing strong actions.

Deciding what you want your audience to do is another way of saying, "choose a powerful objective." Assembling and interpreting the information is about finding actions or tactics that will actually get your audience to do whatever it is you want them to. The reinvented speech process achieves the same organization and clarity as the traditional approach, but it actively addresses the speaker's relationship to the audience and, therefore, will result in a more effective presentation.

Later in this chapter we'll examine each step of the reinvented process in detail. But before you can effectively apply it to your own speech, you need material to work with. It's time to put some thought into what's important about your topic, what type of speech you want to give, and exactly who is going to be hearing it.

FINDING AND FOCUSING MATERIAL

Let's say you're scheduled to give a speech. (If you're not, be an actor and pretend you are!) Perhaps someone (your boss?) has told you what you're supposed to talk about. Maybe it's entirely up to you. In any case, your first step is to define your topic carefully. Instead of asking yourself, "What do I want to talk about?" try wondering, "What might they need to hear about?" Making your audience's needs central to your presentation right from the outset will produce great benefits later on.

As in stating objectives and actions, specificity is crucial at this stage. If you're still at the point where you're saying, "I'm giving some kind of toast at the reception" or "Michaelson wants me to talk about marketing," it's time to get a little more concrete.

Start by thinking about what you might have to offer. Have you been paying special attention to the firm's Web presence? Do you have some outrageous dirt on the groom? You begin with yourself:

your own tastes, knowledge, experiences. And you start to jot some things down. Do it on index cards, one thought per card, so you can easily order your thoughts later.

What kind of things should you jot down? What you think is important about your topic. What your mother thinks is important about the topic. The most exciting, unusual, embarrassing thing you can think of in relation to your topic. Other topics that seem related to this one. Anecdotes that come to mind. In other words, anything.

Do this for a few minutes, then put it aside. Come back to it later and write down a few more things on a few more cards. Don't judge, just write. Leave it again and come back to it later. You want to give your subconscious some time to absorb what you've been coming up with. Take a few cards and a pen with you whenever you leave the house, so you can make a note if something occurs to you at the gas station. Your goal is not to come up with everything you're going to say, just a bunch of possibilities.

One of the most important things this kind of brainstorming can do for you is to show you how much you know. If you let yourself write freely, without worrying whether your ideas are good or bad— silencing your internal critic—you're sure to discover that you know an awful lot related to your topic, no matter what your topic is. That can be very comforting, especially if you were worried you'd have nothing to say. It can also be a little distressing, because eventually you'll come up with so many ideas that you couldn't possibly use them all.

So after you've got a bunch of ideas down, you're going to have to work on focusing them. That means picking and choosing. You do it by looking for patterns in what you've written. (Patterns are going to be a very big part of the process from here on out.) Do a large number of your ideas fall into some category? (Recent trends? Misconceptions? Historical lessons?) Does this category seem to be something that would be of particular interest or value to your audience? You want to search for a *theme* that connects some of your ideas to each other and to your audience and then limit your subject to those ideas. How much you need to limit yourself depends on the length and type of your speech, which we'll address next.

TYPES OF PRESENTATIONS

Speeches come in all shapes and sizes. They can be as short as a twenty-second toast and as long as a full-day formal presentation. Or shorter or longer, for that matter. It all depends on the venue, the audience, and your objectives. If you aren't sure how long you should plan to speak, talk to someone about it. Find out who's organizing the event and ask what's expected of you. It doesn't make much sense to continue preparing until you have at least an estimate for the time.

Another important thing to keep in mind as you proceed is the extent to which you want to prepare the words in advance. Do you plan to speak essentially off the cuff? Refer occasionally to notes? Deliver it verbatim from a typed copy? Memorize a complete text?

Before putting pen to paper or fingers to keyboard, it helps to know what type of presentation you plan to give, so you have a model in mind for how you might structure it. Following are brief descriptions of the basic presentation types and the situations to which each is best suited.

The Impromptu Speech

The impromptu speech is the essentially-off-the-cuff kind. That doesn't necessarily mean no preparation at all, but the preparation is minimal. It's meant to seem as though you haven't really prepared and are making the whole thing up on the spot. You use no notes or text, and you don't memorize anything except possibly a list of major points you want to cover.

A lot of people assume this is necessarily the most desirable type of presentation to give, where you appear able to speak fluidly and eloquently off the top of your head. Some people think signs of preparation like notes or a script will somehow indicate that you're too weak brained to think on your feet. But it all depends on the context.

If you're speaking in a high-stakes situation, it's certainly not ideal to have your audience think you're just coming up with these ideas for the first time. On the other hand, if you're giving a toast and you sound excessively scripted, you'll come off as—at best—excessively scripted.

The impromptu style is best suited to remarks that are casual or not particularly serious and that will last no more than five minutes. If your speech is longer than a few minutes or you think you might not be comfortable with so much ad libbing, the impromptu approach is probably not the best idea.

The skills of impromptu speaking are essential for all speakers, however. No matter how fully prepared your speech is, you'll want to have the flexibility to go off script should the mood strike or the need arise, just as an actor might do if someone forgets a line. Later in this chapter you'll encounter the Chef Exercise, a training tool that encourages the kind of spontaneity required for confident ad libbing.

The Extemporaneous Speech

Although the terms *impromptu* and *extemporaneous* are often used interchangeably, we'll call a speech extemporaneous if it's carefully prepared ahead of time but the exact words are not chosen until the moment of delivery. This category includes speeches that are just slightly more prepared than an impromptu, all the way up to long, highly organized speeches, often presented with the help of note cards.

This type of presentation is appropriate in many contexts, from light and humorous to very serious, as long as a certain level of informality is desirable. The extemporaneous form tends to work best when you have a good deal of latitude with your message (meaning you don't have to stick to the company line word for word), when the audience may expect a certain degree of interactivity in the presentation, and when the setting is fairly intimate. Of course, if you suspect you would not feel secure with only note cards to guide you, you should plan to write out the speech.

The Scripted Speech

As the name suggests, in a scripted speech the words are fully written out in advance, and you bring the text with you to the podium or the table, or memorize it verbatim beforehand. If your message requires extensive backup, involves a complex line of thinking, or would benefit from particularly elegant phrasing, it's probably best to have written out a complete version of the speech as a way of grounding yourself in the specifics. You can always stray from the script in the moment of delivery if it feels right to you.

The biggest potential problem with a fully scripted speech is that it might, if not prepared well, come off sounding stilted, as though it were just being read or recited from rote. Proper text analysis and rehearsal will keep that from happening, as you'll see in later chapters.

KNOWING YOUR AUDIENCE

If you attend a Broadway extravaganza one night and a "play of ideas" in a Greenwich Village basement the next, you'll naturally notice some differences between the two audiences. One will be more conservative, one more avant-garde, one better dressed, one better versed. (You decide which is which.)

Performing one of those plays for the other one's audience would be a big mistake. Many members of the Village audience would find the Broadway show a tasteless capitalist display. The Broadway theatergoers might find the other play pretentious, vulgar, and boring. In either case, the theatrical communication would probably not be received in the way it was intended.

As full partners in the scene you're creating, the audience must receive your careful consideration. As hard as it can be to believe, your speaking engagement is not primarily about you. It's about them. The more energy you put into sounding smart, making a good impression, and getting a promotion, the less likely you are to sound smart, make a good impression, or get a promotion. It's the big paradox of all performance situations. To give a good performance, you cannot be concentrating on giving a good performance.

This is especially true when it comes to public speaking. Your audience isn't there to critique your performance—they've come to learn something, to be convinced, or to get inspired. In fact, if all they remember after you leave the stage is that you were a good speaker, you've failed just as miserably as if they thought you were lousy. No matter how much they like you, if you haven't affected them with your message, you haven't accomplished your primary goal as a speaker. Precisely what effect you want to have and how you might achieve it (your objectives and actions) are specific to your situation and must be carefully thought out, but that can't be done until you take the emphasis off *you* and put it on *them*.

What are their wants and needs, and how do they relate to the possible things you have to say? The answer will be different for each audience, but all audiences will have certain things in common. For one thing, they all want you to talk about them, not about you. They want to feel that you have their interests at heart. So it's helpful if you actually do have their interests at heart.

This is true even if you are presenting a point of view that is in direct opposition to theirs. You will be effective only if you convince them that your point of view will somehow benefit them—if not now, then in the long run. The perennial political debate over paying down the national debt is a great example of this phenomenon. Most Americans would receive a more immediate benefit from a tax break than from reducing the debt, but many politicians have made the argument that, in the big picture, debt reduction is better for the country, the economy, and thus the individual taxpayer. And, by and large, people have bought it.

The success of your speech is directly tied to your success in addressing the needs of your audience. They are sitting there wondering what they are going to get out of it. How will they benefit? Will you show them how to make more money? Earn more respect? Lead a happier life? Maybe just understand or appreciate something or someone in a more fruitful or enjoyable way? Think of the last time you listened to someone give a good speech, and you'll see how universal and fundamental this idea is. It was more about you than it was about the speaker, wasn't it?

Your audience may be people you see every day, total strangers, or something in between. No matter how well you think you know them, you should consider the following questions before spending any more time on what you're going to say:

What is their level of expertise or experience in the topic?

Do you expect them to be interested in the topic?

Which parts of your ideas or knowledge are likely to be new to them?

Will they likely be initially sympathetic, hostile, or indifferent to your message?

Why do they think you're there? What are they expecting?

Are they primarily decision makers or more junior people, and how might that matter?

Are they primarily men or women, and how might that matter?

Are they primarily old or young, and how might that matter?

What problems are they facing? What keeps them up at night?

What objections might they raise to what you have to say?

What is the worst thing that could happen to them if they do not hear your speech?

What is the greatest benefit they might receive from hearing your speech?

What do they most need to hear, and why do they need to hear it?

What response would you most like them to have as they listen to you?

What action would you like them to take immediately after hearing you? The next day? A week later? A month?

Usually the best way to start answering these questions is to talk to people, and the best people to talk to are those in charge of the event. Bother them until they tell you everything you need to know. They'll thank you later.

You can use this newfound information and your new ways of thinking to help you focus the ideas you've been coming up with. You've already faced the fact that you can't tell them everything you know. You now have to face the fact that you shouldn't even necessarily tell them all the parts you like best.

Speech guru Dale Carnegie says a listener's mind can't take in more than four or five main points in thirty minutes—and he's right. So no matter how long your speech is, you want to make sure you're focusing on the content that is most likely to strike a chord with your audience. Look back at your brainstormed ideas and think about which parts these particular people most need to hear.

Once you know a lot about the audience, you may discover there are things you need to know about your topic. Now's the time to start filling in information by doing a little research, if necessary. You want, as much as possible, to be an expert on your topic, so people will have plenty of reason to listen to you. (Make sure you've limited your topic to the point where reasonable mastery of the material is possible.) If there are numbers to back up one of your ideas, but you don't know what they are—find out. If your story would benefit from knowing the name of the bride's nursery school sweetheart—find out. No need to go overboard, but you'll want to have as many specifics as possible at your disposal before trying to structure the speech.

THE CHEF EXERCISE

It may seem early, but once you've generated some note cards and given some thought to your audience, it's time to actually start saying some words out loud.

Here's an acting exercise that's great for finding out where you stand at this stage and what you need to concentrate on as you continue. It's got two steps. One addresses general public speaking skills and the other applies directly to the speech at hand.

It goes like this: You pick a topic you know next to nothing about—Japanese art, French cooking, physics, whatever. You then assign yourself the role of expert on that subject. If you know nothing about automotive maintenance, you've just landed a job as an auto mechanic. If you choose cooking as your topic, you become a chef—hence the name of the game.

Go ahead and pick a topic you're hopeless in. Now imagine we've called you in to give a presentation on this topic.

It sounds impossible. What could you possibly say, right?

Wrong. It's an acting exercise. Use your imagination. You've been called to speak in front of a group of people who are ready and willing to believe that you're an expert. Those people are in need of information, and you're going to give it to them.

Make the topic specific. If you've chosen cooking, imagine you've been asked to discuss the menu at your new restaurant. If it's Japanese art, you're here to address recent trends. If it's automotive maintenance, tell us what to do when something starts clanging under the hood.

You can do this alone if you like, but it's much more valuable with somebody listening, so recruit a friend. Plan to speak for two full minutes—and really take it seriously. Leave the room and return as the expert ready to solve all our problems. Pretend you've spent hours preparing. Do your best to convince us you're the one in the know.

Here's the most important part: Keep going. Don't stop to judge yourself. Don't give yourself away by hemming and hawing, laughing, looking away, or otherwise "breaking character." As impossible as this sounds, if you commit to it, you'll find you have something to say and can actually say it with authority.

Give it a try.

❖   ❖   ❖

NOW HERE'S WHAT PROBABLY HAPPENED TO YOU AS YOU DID THE CHEF Exercise: You hemmed and hawed, laughed, looked away, and otherwise "broke character." Sometimes you lied outrageously and gave demonstrably bad advice. There were moments when you felt like such an impostor that you couldn't think of anything to say. Or maybe you didn't even bother doing the exercise because it seemed so pointless.

But if you tried it and can manage not to be too hard on yourself, you can probably identify moments when you discovered that there was *something* believable and somewhat expertlike that you could say. Maybe you told us we should get regular automotive checkups. Or that a very popular feature of your new menu was going to be the special chocolate sauce that would be served with every single dessert. Maybe these are not brilliant ideas, but if you found a way to believe in them as you spoke, you're on your way to mastering the art of keeping going, which is priceless.

If you think you could do a better job with a second chance, give yourself sixty more seconds and go for it.

Most people who try the Chef Exercise find they can be more successful at it than they ever expected. It may be hard to fight the tendency to censor and judge yourself, but a little practice with this exercise will prove to you that you have the ability (because everybody has it) to speak with authority, even on a topic that you know nothing about.

Now let's use this exercise as a tool for developing your speech.

The topic is now the one you will actually be speaking on. Assign yourself the role of expert in the field. (You may, of course, actually *be* an expert in this field, but even if you're not, pretend you are.) Think a bit about who will (or might) be in your audience for this speech, and pick an objective, something you want to get that audience to do as a result of listening to you. (This doesn't have to be the "right" objective, just something to give you a reason to speak.) Now give yourself anywhere from one minute to ten, but no more, to give a complete speech on your topic. Don't expect it to be anything like what you'll actually end up delivering to a real audience. It's still just the Chef Exercise. Your job is to imagine that your audience has expressed a need to understand something, and you're going to pursue your objective with utter authority, in complete sentences, with no stammering or other giveaways, as though you're supremely prepared and there's nothing you'd rather do than give this speech.

This time, get a tape recorder out and record whatever you come up with.

Go.

THINK OF THE SPEECH YOU'VE JUST RECORDED AS YOUR FIRST DRAFT. No need to listen to it right away (some people hate the sound of their own voice so much that it can be debilitating) but go ahead if you dare. Or put the tape in a safe place to come back to at a later time if you change your mind. If you don't choose to listen to it now, just think back over what you said.

It was unstructured, naturally. You've given no attention so far to the idea of structure. It was a ramble, and that's what it was supposed to be.

It's very likely that what you said is a strong indicator of what you think the major issues of your speech should be. You probably said several things you never expected to say, and you may be surprised to discover some good ideas in there, or a particularly felicitous turn of phrase. That's gold. Forget the mud that may have been hiding it; wash it down the stream and collect the good stuff.

Take some notes on ideas, connections, examples, or phrases

that you'd like to save from this experiment. If you think it went particularly well, transcribe the whole thing from the tape and use it as an outline to work from.

STRUCTURING YOUR SPEECH

Now that you've got a base from which to work, let's return to the speech development process described at the beginning of the chapter. As you'll recall, the three steps for constructing a truly persuasive speech are:

1. Decide what you want your audience to do.

2. Assemble the information they must have in order to do it.

3. Interpret the information in a way that persuades them to do it.

You are now ready to apply this process to the speech you are creating. Let's look at each step in detail.

1. Decide What You Want Your Audience to Do.

Write down some possibilities for the main thing you want to achieve. Which one seems strongest to you? Is it achievable? (It's okay to aim high.) Is it specific? How can you strengthen it? Don't settle for merely getting the audience to nod or applaud. Pick something really active like: *I want them to race to the phones to start implementing the new practices I've just described.*

This will be your "superobjective," and it should take the form, "I want them to_____." When you've formulated your superobjective and are certain that it's specific, potentially achievable, and as strong as you can make it, write it out on a clean piece of paper and keep it in view.

Next: What other objectives do you hope to achieve along the way to your superobjective? There are probably many. Before they can race to those phones, you may need to get them to respect your opinion, to understand the long-term consequences of the status quo, to make the correct decision about which policy to implement first, etc. Write your secondary objectives out on a separate piece of paper.

2. Assemble the Information They Must Have in Order to Do It.
    Look through your note cards. Now that you have strong objectives in mind, which facts and ideas seem integral and which seem extraneous? Dump the extraneous ones. (Make a pile of extraneous cards and label it EXTRANE-OUS, or, better yet, throw them away.)

Of the facts and ideas you want to keep, some will naturally gravitate toward each other. Reasons for a decrease in the number of teenage pregnancies will be intimately related to the *statistics* on teenage pregnancies, for example. Make piles of cards that seem to be related to each other. Have as many or as few piles as you like. If new ideas come to mind, write them down on some fresh cards and find a pile to put them in.

Do you find you have a certain number of major issues, with subissues attached? Make some subpiles. Which cards relate to which objectives? Does this relationship suggest a helpful way of grouping them?

Throughout this process it's important to keep in mind that there is no right way to do it; therefore, there's no wrong way to do it. As in any creative endeavor, it's all about possibilities. Everything can be rearranged later, so there's nothing to fear. Throw some piles together.

3. Interpret the Information in a Way That Persuades Them to Do It.

Look at your list of objectives. For each one, brainstorm an action or series of actions that might help you achieve it. For example, the objective "I want to get them to support my charity for needy children" might suggest the following actions: enrage them about the plight of a disadvantaged child, frighten them with the consequences of indifference, excite them with promising results from a pilot program, ask them to give money. (Sometimes a direct appeal is the best action of all!) Write down every tactic that comes to mind— no editing allowed.

A SPEECH IN THREE ACTS

Now that you've defined your objectives and considered your actions, you've got to put it all together in a cogent, meaningful way by giving some attention to the form your presentation will take. Even though there are many kinds of speeches, almost all the good ones can be broken down into a beginning, a middle, and an end. That sounds simplistic, but it's the classic three-act dramatic structure that Aristotle championed in the *Poetics* a couple of millennia ago, and it still can't be beat. In theatrical terms, the three acts are sometimes referred to as the exposition, the rising action (which culminates in the climax), and the denouement. In public speaking they're usually called the introduction, the body, and the conclusion.

It's important to understand the main "plot" of your speech in some detail before you can decide how to introduce or conclude it. So we'll deal with Act 2, the middle of the speech, first.

The Body

The body of the speech is the part where you tell the audience what they need to hear and help them understand that information in such a way that they will do what you want them to do. In some ways, the form is as important as the content in achieving your objective. With that in mind, it's time to start organizing your ideas into patterns of thought.

ROADMAPPING

A fundamental mathematical reality underlies the process of speech-making: Information + Information + Information = 0.

Too many speakers operate under the false assumption that Information + Information + Information = Something of Value. They state an idea and support that idea. Then state another idea and support that one. And on it goes. What's missing is the pattern way in which these ideas and supportive interpretations relate to each other and to the objectives of the speaker. It's about *connections*. Don't expect the audience to connect the dots themselves. They won't. You need to first *create* the connections you want them to see, and then find a way to make sure they see them.

We're talking about the highest-level structuring, outlining, or roadmapping of the body of your speech. The forest, not the trees. The master plan. So far it doesn't exist, but it's time to take a stab at it.

It's time to make your first outline—but not the Roman numeral kind. Choose a possible order for your piles of index cards, and jot down some notes about why you might want to order them this way.

Don't think of it as a recipe or blueprint but as a representation of your first thoughts about how the pieces of this puzzle might fit together. Don't spend a lot of time on it at this stage. Just use it as a chance to see what your subconscious has been thinking about the most salient connections it's possible to make among the jumble of parts.

The order of the cards is your outline. Expect this order to change. You'll probably want to do a lot of adding and deleting and shuffling as you strengthen the organization of the speech. Imagine yourself as a tour guide trying to find the most helpful route to take. You're trying to build the strongest possible sense of what the large parts of your journey will be, what the smaller parts are along the way, and exactly how each part relates to every other part.

PROVEN PATTERNS

If you can identify a strong pattern that explains why you or-dered your piles the way you did, and if it applies to every single pile, you may have already hit on your ideal structure. If you can't explain it yet, you probably need to think more deeply about the possible connections.

There are also, of course, many tried-and-true organizing struc-tures that you can use in pursuit of your superobjective. Here are a few of the most common:

Problem and solution. In this structure you provide a clear pic-ture of a problem, then present the steps to its solution.

Chronological order. If the historical development of a phenom-enon seems to play an important role, you might be able to achieve your objective by analyzing changes from some be-ginning point to the present.

Good news–bad news. Would it be helpful to compare positives and negatives throughout your speech? Similar organizational structures include old–new, us–them, present–future, and in-novations–status quo.

Extended metaphor. Can you find an image that ties your ideas together and augments their collective meaning? The forest as the speech, the trees as the ideas, the roots as the supporting arguments, the oxygen as the benefits produced, for example.

Of course, you may discover or invent a structure of your own. What you're looking for is a pattern that encompasses everything you want your audience to understand and at the same time helps them understand it.

TACTICS

Once you have a sense of the high-level structure of your speech—the skeleton—you need to start fleshing it out with specific actions. Begin by picking one of the actions you brainstormed earlier (see p. 28), say, "to stroke their egos for a job well done." Decide where in your speech you want to perform that action. Then look at your cards. Which of them lend themselves to that action? Maybe you'll find a card about an increase in sales resulting from a massive team effort. You can certainly use that information to stroke their egos.

Also look back at your list of objectives. Do you think you'll be able to achieve them all with the material you've assembled? You may find that you haven't brainstormed enough strong actions to do a good job of pursuing your goals. Here are some effective tactics to add to your repertoire:

Statistics

If interpreted helpfully, a few dramatic numbers are worth their weight in gold. They have the twang of irrefutable fact.

Choose the most startling statistics you can find. Of course, you need to make sure your numbers are correct, and you need to put them in a context that interprets their value for the audience. Give your source whenever you think it will bolster your credibility, and play with the numbers to find the best form to present them in.

With all statistics, the idea should be to imprint an image on the audience's mind. Sometimes it's more meaningful to say revenue increased by 38 percent; sometimes it's stronger to say it increased by $4.5 million. (But in most cases you don't want to use the exact number: $4,502,341 is much less memorable.) Or maybe the audience will get the picture better if you note that this year's increase in revenue is greater than the last two years' increases combined. Or show that if revenue were to continue to increase at this rate, in five years the company would have increased its revenue eightfold.

Be creative and use your numbers to make a lasting impression on your listeners. Bottom line: If you've got a nice figure, flaunt it!

Personal Examples

Almost every speech, from the most inspirational to the most businesslike, will benefit from the injection of something personal. The whole reason you're speaking instead of mailing out an essay is so that the audience can benefit from your human interpretation and commitment to the material. You can strengthen your connection to the audience (and hence their connection to you) by including things that no one but you could include. The personal touch will also make the speech more fun for both you and your listeners.

Does part of your material remind you of a story? Of course, the real answer to this question is: Probably not. Speakers are always saying, "That reminds me of a story." But that doesn't mean that the hilarious tale of the birthday picnic gone awry just popped into that speaker's head the moment he decided to talk about the history of Indo-European languages. It's always nice to have a relevant personal story to tell, but it probably won't materialize of its own accord. You're going to have to look for the personal connection.

Begin by asking yourself how your topic affects you personally. If your first answer is that it doesn't affect you personally at all, don't accept that. Search for a connection. If you're talking about international banking, your experiences at the corner ATM may shed a lot of unexpected light. If you're doing a presentation for a bunch of banking vice presidents, don't forget that they use ATMs, too.

In addition to thinking about how the topic relates to your life, try thinking about how your life relates to the topic. Dale Carnegie recommends looking back over significant events in your life and asking yourself if there are lessons that apply. It also helps to stay open to inspiration as you live your daily life. If you go to the grocery store during the time you're working on your speech, have a look around. Maybe the length of the checkout lines will suggest something about product distribution channels. Remember, your audience goes to the grocery store. Try to find a story that will engage them on a personal level and give them a new angle from which to view a part of your message.

That's the purpose of any story you tell. You're using your own experience as an example of the universal human experience. The reason your frustration at the ATM may be worth telling is because it may make your audience *identify* with you. You're building a human bond and illuminating your material at the same time.

In most cases, you are not the topic of the speech. Therefore, personal stories that do not help you achieve your objective are inappropriate. Make sure that any story you choose to tell is directly relevant to the issue at hand, and do everything you can to make that relevance crystal clear.

Other Stories

You can, of course, tell stories that you've heard somewhere or read in the newspaper in addition to events and observations from your own life. All the above comments about the need to make it relevant and to use the story to connect with the audience still apply. In a way, any story you use should be thought of as a personal story. Find your personal connection to it.

For example, say you decide to talk about the time George Bush the elder fell off the stage. (We'll assume you have some good reason for doing so.) What's your personal stake in that story? Did you find it funny? Embarrassing? Troubling? How did you first hear about it? Why do you think it struck such a chord with *you* that you decided to tell it? The more you can let us in on your own relationship to any story you tell, the more we'll be interested in hearing it.

Humor

Okay, stop me if you've heard this one.

You should include moments of humor. That goes for business presentations, lectures, even (and maybe especially) eulogies. (And no, we're not joking.) No matter how serious you think your message is, a little lightness will make your speech more effective. Maybe you can get away without it if you're giving the State of the Union address or announcing the bombing of Pearl Harbor, but for most nonpresidential speaking assignments, humor is a must.

It can soften controversy and relieve tension. It can get the audience's attention back if they're drifting. And, most important, it can make them like you.

Everyone enjoys spending time with someone who has a sense of humor, and if the audience enjoys spending time with you, you'll have a much better chance of achieving your objective than if they don't.

Many speakers worry that they don't know how to be funny.

We'll deal with issues of how to deliver humorous material later in the book, but if you're approaching humor in the right way, you'll see that it's not necessarily about having a lampshade-on-your-head personality or a magical proficiency at telling jokes. The most important and effective humor is small. It's about finding the light or ironic side of a comment, letting your audience know that you're not taking yourself too seriously. It can be as small as a smile of understanding, a metaphorical wink that says, "We've all been *there*!"

These little moments take many forms.

Self-deprecation, if sincere, is a wonderful way to lighten up the proceedings. If you can make fun of yourself a little bit, you'll gain respect for being sure of yourself and unself-conscious.

Don't be afraid to use quirky or unusual facts because you think they're not dignified enough. Big Bird's exact height just may turn out to be useful information for your audience of poultry farmers.

Juxtapose incongruities. Mix metaphors. Heighten ironies. Reinvent clichés. Exaggerate. Understate. Alliterate. Rhyme. Dare to glimpse the silly side. If you let them know that you get it, however minor *it* is, you'll strengthen the audience's sense that you're really with them, understanding how they're hearing what you're saying. Even when these moments of lightness haven't been consciously written into a speech, they're always there if you look for them; and if you miss them, the audience will notice on some level and wonder why you didn't see the funny side.

By keeping an eye out for these little opportunities, you can get plenty of humor into a speech without telling a single joke. But maybe you like to tell jokes, or feel, for one reason or another, that a joke would strengthen your presentation. By all means, use one.

If you do decide to tell a real joke, first of all make sure it makes a relevant point. It's also important of course to pick one that you think is funny, that to your knowledge is not well known, and that is appropriate to your speaking venue—but its relevance to your message should be your top concern.

An actor approaching a comic script is always wary of jokes that are unrelated to character and situation and seem to be there only to get the laugh. Sometimes they get the laugh, of course, but sometimes they don't, and if the joke doesn't serve some other, more integral purpose, it can hang you out to dry. On the other hand, if the joke says something about the character, relates to a theme, or furthers the plot, failure to get the laugh is no catastrophe.

The same is true for you. No joke can bomb if it makes a point.

The way to make a point with a joke is to set up an analogy. That chicken is really crossing the road of, say, your company's destiny. Whatever the connection is, make sure you do everything in your power to make sure the analogy is clear.

Even if the joke gets nary a titter, if the analogy is clear and valid, it has served an important purpose and no one will fault you for not being funny enough. If it does get a laugh, that's icing on the cake. But if you don't do a good job of connecting the joke to a larger thought, they may love you for making them laugh, but that's all they'll remember. You've upstaged your message. And if by some fluke they don't find it funny, you'll be dyin' up there.

If you'd like to tell a joke but don't know where to find one, start paying more attention to the numerous funny things you hear every day on television and in real life, and steal them. Every time a sitcom makes you laugh, ask yourself if there's any way in which the joke could analogize a point in your speech. If you do a lot of public speaking, it's a good idea to keep a notebook of jokes that strike you funny and look through it every time you write a speech, searching for analogies. You might also want to look at *Reader's Digest,* the Comedy Channel, *The New Yorker,* newspaper columns, and the Internet. Or call a couple of your funniest friends and ask them to make you laugh. Take their jokes very seriously and take lots of notes.

Other Devices

Examples Use lots of examples. Especially if you have a good deal of abstract information to impart, your audience will long for concrete illustrations of the material's applicability or its relevance to their own lives. If they don't get a clear sense of how your ideas work in practice, they'll tune out.

Questions Ask the audience questions. Even in a fully written-out speech, taking time to get feedback from the audience, even if it's just a show of hands, benefits you in at least three ways: It lets them know you care about their thoughts and experiences, it provides a change of pace, and it gives you information that may help you focus the rest of the speech more precisely on the audience's needs.

Quotes Quote an authority. Or quote a non-authority who happened to say something witty or incisive about your topic. (Check out *Bartlett's Familiar Quotations* and other collections, books by visionaries in your field, even local and national news programs.) Go on to help your listeners interpret the quotation the way you want them to.

Suspense Can you find an artful way to keep them guessing a bit? Maybe you withhold a crucial detail in your description of an event, or drop in cryptic comments here and there that end up making perfect sense by the end of the speech. This very dramatic device can do a lot to keep your audience with you, but it works only if there's a good payoff. Even if you don't go for the super-suspenseful, it's a good idea to find some kind of buildup to your presentation so that you reach your most powerful material—the climax—just as the body of the speech is ending and you're moving into your conclusion.

Of course, all these tactics are merely ideas. You may come up with wonderful ways of your own to pursue your objective with clarity, power, and gusto. The main thing is to look for as many different ways to get through to your audience as possible. Saw a woman in half if you think it will help.

The Introduction

Act 1 is where we meet the characters, pick up some necessary background, and set the plot in motion—and there's no time to dillydally. A vague or drawn-out introduction can keep you from ever gaining an audience's respect or sympathy, no matter how great the rest of your performance turns out to be.

The opening is generally considered the most difficult part of a speech, and with good reason. It's probably the part where you'll be the most nervous. You have no momentum. You may not yet be accustomed to the room, the lighting, the faces staring at you. You may find yourself needing to concentrate on things unrelated to your message, like transitioning out of the previous presenter's talk or getting an unruly audience's attention. And it's true that first impressions are important.

That's not meant to scare you. All those obstacles are easily overcome (and will be specifically addressed in later chapters). But they show how important it is to take special care in crafting your introduction. Even if you're speaking extemporaneously, you should prepare your introduction in detail.

If no one introduces you, you'll have to introduce yourself. Give them exactly as much information as they'll need in order to trust your authority and know who you are in relation to them. Then move on.

Here is what the introduction to your speech must do: It must state clearly and directly what specific issue you will be addressing, explain how you will address it, and convince the audience that they should care. If you do those three things creatively and succinctly, you're off to a great start.

Many speakers, perhaps in an attempt to win points for modesty, choose to begin with some kind of apology. This is a mistake. If you do it, you're undermining yourself from the very beginning. Yet the temptation can be terribly strong to say something like, "Thank you so much for taking time out of your busy schedules to be here today. I promise not to take too much of your time." It's certainly polite, but it suggests that there are a whole lot more productive things your audience could be doing than listening to you. Even if that's true, it's not the message you want uppermost in their minds at the top of the show.

So how's this instead? "I'm here to talk about the importance of home smoke detectors. I will enumerate the benefits of having one in every room, go on to tell a few horror stories, and finish by discussing the relative merits of several different brands. You should care because your lives are at stake."

Well, not very good.

It's succinct and it gets in the basic information we need, but the creative element is missing. This speaker has told us what he has to offer, but he hasn't reached across those footlights to grab our attention with something that appeals to our humanity. As a result, although this introduction *tells* us we should care, it does not *convince* us to care, and thus fails in one of the most important jobs of any introduction.

A better approach might be to start right off with one of those horror stories. That would pull us right in by appealing to our emotions. The speaker could then go on to give a brief roadmap of his talk, then plunge in. All the requirements of a good introduction would be met, and we would have good reason to pay attention to the rest of what he had to say.

Although you don't want to be overly showy, you do want to grab the audience's attention right from the top. You can do this with a story, an amazing statistic, references to the audience's specific situation (we love to hear about ourselves), a controversial comment, an arresting visual, or a particularly relevant and funny joke. Take stock of your own personality and goals and decide how you would most like to begin.

Giving your audience a roadmap is uniquely relevant if your presentation is long or especially complicated. They'll be able to take in the information a lot more efficiently if they understand the framework ahead of time.

Once you've grabbed their attention and roadmapped, move right on into the main action: Act 2, the body of the speech.

The Conclusion

Act 2 ends with your most persuasive material—the climax. All that's really left to do is to make sure they know what action you want them to take in response to everything they've heard. Send them out into the world armed with new information and a plan for the future.

Of course, if your speech is a toast, the call to action may be nothing more than "Please lift your glasses . . ." More complex speeches may require more complex responses from the audience, but the conclusion is the time to distill your message down to its purest, most easily remembered form.

It might help to review the main points of the speech so that one of the last things they hear is a succinct set of reasons why they should take action. You can also provide a nice sense of closure by referring back to your opening. For example, "What happened to the Petersons does not have to happen to you. Please install a fire alarm in every room and test them regularly."

As with the introduction, it's best not to leave the conclusion to chance. Prepare it carefully, so you can be in total control of your audience's final impression. If you're unprepared, you're likely to say something clichéd and ineffective like, "Well, in closing . . ." or "I see our time is up" or "I guess that's it." Give plenty of thought ahead of time to how you want to signal that the end is near (and make sure the end really is near when you do) and let the last line be your most authoritative and confident of the whole presentation: "Your children's lives can be saved for less than $85 a year."

Write "Thank you" on a note card and put it on the bottom of your last pile, and you've got yourself a speech.

WRITING WITH STYLE

When it comes to choosing specific words, the sheer number of possibilities can stop a writer in his tracks. It's called writer's block, and it's really just stage fright before you even get to the stage. One nice thing about speeches as opposed to other forms of writing, though, is that your listeners won't have much chance to go back and study your word choices. Once you say them, they're gone. That's why stumbling over a word here and there is not the terrible problem people tend to think it is, and it also means that you don't have to agonize over every word in the writing stage. You don't have to be Shakespeare to write a good speech.

Still, of course, you want to use your words as powerfully as you can, since they're your most effective tool in affecting your audience. If you're planning to write out some or all of your presentation, the issue of style is going to come up. How technical, how florid, how quirky do you want to be? All speakers are different, as are all speaking occasions, but a few general principles might be helpful.

First of all, try to approximate the way you talk. It can be tempting to use highfalutin words and phrases in writing that you would never actually say aloud. A little bit of that is okay, because you want your speech to be more effective than everyday chat, but don't stray too much in the direction of high rhetoric.

Simplicity is the key. You want to be clear and direct. Vary the lengths of your sentences, but keep most of them short. Use as little technical jargon as you can get away with, and be sure to define any term the audience could possibly be unfamiliar with. Don't worry about grammatical "errors" like ending sentences with prepositions. Even though much of the material may be old hat to you, keep the language fresh by concentrating on how new the ideas will be to your audience.

If you're writing your own speech as well as delivering it, you're playwright as well as actor. Keep the sense of play! It's okay to be a little dramatic. Vivify your presentation with strong verbs (like *vivify* and *banish*). Banish the passive voice. (Never say "Chicago was outranked by New York" when you could say "New York outranked Chicago.") Keep in mind at all times that your goal is to *persuade*. Aim at your listeners' emotions as well as their intellects.

VISUALS

A chandelier crashing to the stage. An alien riding a bicycle over the treetops. The White House exploding before your eyes. Some of the most memorable moments in plays and movies fall into the category of visual effects.

A public presentation, like any theatrical event, is a visual experience as well as an aural one. Visual aids can give a boost to almost any kind of speech. You probably don't want to blow anything up, but it's important in the early stages of working on a presentation to start thinking about whether or not you want to show slides or other auxiliary materials, and what kinds might best suit your message and situation.

Too many speakers use aids for the wrong reasons. The most prevalent wrong reason is because it seems to be the thing to do. Slides have become virtually indispensable to most large business presentations. Does anyone ever dare turn the projector off?

Our culture is full of visual stimuli, and it's true that audiences may be coming to expect something to look at (other than you) as they listen to a presentation. But don't put together a big slide show just because everybody else is doing it, or you may end up with extraneous or confusing materials that detract rather than aid. As *Star Wars* director George Lucas once said, "A special effect is a tool, a means of telling a story. A special effect without a story is a pretty boring thing." It's completely possible to do a dazzling presentation relying on human presence and the spoken word alone, and in many cases it might be a refreshing change of pace.

But there are, of course, many good reasons to use visual aids, depending on the situation. If done well they can add liveliness and variety. They improve retention, because people are more likely to remember things that they see as well as hear. And some information is most effectively expressed in visual form. Just remember that you're the star of this show and you don't want to be upstaged by an overhead projection.

With that in mind, it makes sense that your visual materials should be as simple as possible. They should look professional, of course, but producing a music video on your topic is almost always going too far.

On the other hand, typing portions of your script onto slides is not going far enough. To be effective, visual aids should exploit their visual nature. Use pictures, diagrams, and graphs that clarify or give depth to your ideas. Shapes, colors, sizes, and relative positions of the objects in your picture all have meaning. If the most important thing on a slide is the words, then it's not an effective slide, and you'll be better off without it.

Yes, visual aids can detract from the effectiveness of your speech—or even ruin it altogether. One of the speaker's big jobs is to maintain and focus the audience's attention, so each and every visual brings with it a liability: It forces the audience to split its attention between you and the picture. An aid is only valuable if the benefits of the visual nature of the information are enough to outweigh that liability. As you work on your speech, it's important to develop visuals that you can work *with*, and won't have to work *against*.

The most common type of visual aid for large presentations is the good old slide, sometimes made with a camera, sometimes with a computer. But there are lots of other kinds to consider. Flip charts, handouts, overheads, models, maps, and dry-erase boards all have something to recommend them, depending on the venue and your objectives. Just remember to keep it as simple as possible, and use aids only when words are not enough.

Rather than developing your script and then adding visuals or developing visuals and then adding a script, it's best to work on them simultaneously. Changes in one will necessitate changes in the other, and you want to be sure they will operate hand in hand.

If an art department, a design consultant, or anyone else besides you will be producing your slides, keep as much control as you can. Find out ahead of time how much input you'll have concerning the overall "look," a date when you can expect to have your visuals completed so that you can rehearse with them, and how easy or difficult it will be to make corrections and other changes if they become necessary.

FLEXIBILITY

An unfortunate truth about any kind of live performance is that things rarely go exactly as planned. When you actually get around to giving your speech, you may well find that although the organizers of the event told you you'd have forty-five minutes, they have decided to give you only half an hour. Or some cantankerous audience member may continually interrupt you with questions, even though you asked them to save questions for the end. The spontaneity is all part of the fun!

In case of these or other unforeseen circumstances, it's nice to have a little flexibility built into the structure of your speech. Prepare a little more material than you actually plan to use—a few more examples or stories, an extra insight or two. Decide where you might insert them if you're asked to speak longer than you expected. Conversely, try to identify self-contained pieces of the script that you could cut if they shorten your allotted time.

EDITING

Alfred Hitchcock had some good advice for writers: "Drama is life with the dull bits cut out."

Once you have a good draft of your speech, set it aside for a day or two, then come back to it armed with metaphorical scissors. It's time to nip and tuck, maybe a little, maybe a lot.

Carefully read through everything you've written and ask yourself these questions:

Is the topic narrow enough to be addressed thoroughly in the given time?

Does the speech have a clear objective?

Do you still believe in both the overall message and the details?

Is the speech oriented toward the needs of the audience?

Is it too long, too short, or just right?

Does it have a clear beginning, middle, and end?

Does the introduction grab the audience's attention?

Have any parts revealed themselves to be extraneous or repetitive?

Is the information verifiably accurate?

Are there enough light moments?

Is the organizing structure readily discernible?

Does the speech employ a wide variety of tactics in pursuit of the objective?

Does it adequately reflect your personal commitment to the message?

Is the language simple, clear, active, and appropriate to the context?

Does the body of the speech build to a climax?

Is the call to action clear and strong?

Have you built in enough flexibility?

Is the whole speech as persuasive as it could possibly be?

If you've answered all these questions thoughtfully and honestly, you know what areas of your speech need work. Pretend you're a playwright, mercilessly cutting and revising your work in the weeks before the critics arrive. Shuffle those cards, get out your thesaurus and your red pen, and make it better! Be hard on yourself. (It's easier than having an audience be hard on you later.)

When professional writers talk about editing, they use a phrase reminiscent of Medea: "Kill your babies." They mean even though you may be in love with an idea or a turn of phrase, if it does not serve the speech as a whole, it has to die.

Don't stop cutting, pasting, and rewriting until you have the speech you want to give. Once you can be happy with your answers to the questions listed on the previous page, you're ready to start rehearsing.

Chapter 4

Early Rehearsals

"I did it the same way I learned to skate—by doggedly making a fool of myself until I got used to it."

—GEORGE BERNARD SHAW, *on learning to give a speech*

PENCILS DOWN

Congratulations. You've written a speech. You've brainstormed and researched, defined clear objectives, polished each phrase and honed each anecdote. Maybe it's not yet "I Have a Dream," but it's pretty darned good.

Now what? Well, here's what *not* to do: Don't decide the real work is done and tuck it away in a drawer until the day before your presentation. Writing the speech is just a small part of your job as a speaker.

In this chapter you'll begin a structured rehearsal process that will help you get your speech off the page and into the hearts and minds of your listeners. You'll also learn a variety of techniques for communicating your message with commitment and enthusiasm.

REHEARSAL BASICS

Aristotle once said, "We are what we repeatedly do. Excellence therefore is not an act but a habit."

It's a lesson that hasn't been lost on modern-day actors. On average, an actor spends four weeks, thirty-six hours a week, rehearsing for a show that will last no longer than two hours and a role that may be no more than fifty or a hundred lines. That's because actors know that rehearsal—and lots of it—is the only sure road to mastery of a script. Public speakers, on the other hand, tend to think of rehearsal as "going over it in my head once or twice on the plane." Many speakers never even say the words of the script out loud until they're standing in front of an audience. But thinking about your speech and practicing it are two very different things: getting the words in your head does not prepare you to communicate them with your whole being. Only by repeatedly doing your speech—in other words, undertaking a solid rehearsal process—can you develop the habits of excellence.

So what exactly is rehearsal? People unfamiliar with the craft of theater often assume it's about getting the lines of the script down pat. Memorization, however, is just a small part of what actors do, and something they're expected to accomplish on their own time. What actually happens in rehearsal is far more interesting. As any professional actor will tell you, real rehearsal is all about exploration and discovery.

For speakers as well as actors, good rehearsal means exploring the dramatic possibilities of a script—not only what you're saying, but why you're saying it and how you're using your body and voice to powerfully affect your listeners. It also means discovering new meanings in your words and developing enthusiasm for your message.

A good rehearsal process is a lot like breaking in a new pair of jeans. You stretch the material in every conceivable way so that, when you actually have to wear it in public, it'll fit you like a comfortable second skin.

Run Your Mouth

There are many different types of speech rehearsal, some formal, some very informal. Some rehearsal sessions involve doing a mock performance in front of your peers or supervisors; others require nothing more than a few minutes of creative visualization or a friend's willing ear.

You can even rehearse in front of people without anyone knowing you're doing it. The next time you're out with friends, find an opportunity to talk about your topic. Don't let anyone know you're practicing your speech; just go for creating lively conversation. Try to get your companions interested in your subject matter and persuade them of your point of view. Take mental notes about which points in your speech seem particularly persuasive and which ones need some goosing. The more you practice incorporating your thoughts and feelings about your topic into your daily conversation, the more natural you'll feel when you actually take the stage. So seize every opportunity to say the words of your speech out loud, when you're in a crowd or even when you're just a party of one.

Now, if you're like most people, you probably feel silly talking to yourself. Ditto for talking to the wall in your living room or the dog napping on the sofa. And if that's what you do when you rehearse alone you *should* feel silly, because your speech is not intended for yourself or the dog and certainly not for the wall (even if it does have ears).

Since the primary concern of the public speaker is to affect the audience, any effective rehearsal scenario must allow for interaction with either real or imagined listeners. Self-consciousness—the literal kind, too much consciousness of the self—gets in the way of true interaction. At this stage your mind is full of the work *you've* done, the thoughts *you've* had, the mistakes *you've* made. To be an effective speaker you have to get out of your head. And the best way to get out of your head is to get into someone else's.

In other words, you've got to make the audience a big part of every rehearsal, whether there's anyone else in the room with you or not.

Break Down the Wall

As we've said before, there's a fundamental difference between an audience that comes to hear a speech and one that comes to see a play. In the public speaking setting, the audience is an active partner in the scene rather than a group of disinterested onlookers.

In a play, it's often desirable for performers to erect "the fourth wall"—an imaginary barrier between the audience and the stage. This allows actors to concentrate on interacting with each other rather than sending their energy directly out to the audience. The fourth wall gives the audience the illusion that they are peeking in on something private, which is, after all, one of the big draws of going to the theater.

But in public speaking there can be no wall between you and your listeners, because they are not even really an audience, at least not in the traditional passive sense. They are major players. Rather than performing a *monologue for* them, you are engaging in a *dialogue with* them. You're there to address their unvoiced questions and concerns, to solve some of their problems, and to use all the tactics at your disposal to make them respond the way you want them to. All in all, a very interactive relationship.

A lot of public speakers keep a fourth wall firmly in place, because it can feel safer behind it. The trouble is, if you protect yourself in a little bubble at the podium, you will survive the experience but you will not be a success. Shutting yourself off from the audience is the same as shutting yourself off from the potential power of your presentation.

That's because great speaking is as much about reacting as it is about acting. You're speaking not to hear the sound of your own voice, but to get a response from your listeners—so you've got to pay attention to your audience and *care* about the response you're getting. The actions you perform can be deemed successful only if they affect your listeners in the way you intended. If not, you've got to be willing to change those actions to achieve the objectives you are pursuing in your speech.

You Say Potato . . .

Consider this scenario: You work for a toy company that's about to implement radical new practices in product manufacturing. You've been asked to inform a group of subordinates about the changes. Your objective is to get them excited about the innovations being introduced, innovations that not only will make your toys better and safer but also will simplify the lives of the employees producing them and boost company sales. You decide on some appropriate actions to help you achieve this objective: Start with a humorous story about the time your old equipment failed and all the Mr. Potato Heads shrunk to the size of a peanut, move on to a thorough explanation of how fast and easy the new high-tech machines will be, finish by presenting a bar graph showing profits way up in the next year.

Sounds like a pretty good plan, on paper at least. Only, when you actually address your employees, you haven't even gotten two minutes into it and you start to notice something weird: Where you expected them to laugh, they only slump down in their chairs; where you thought they would nod enthusiastically, their eyes glaze over. They're not taking any notes, so how could they possibly remember any of this later on? When you finish, you open it up for questions and are greeted with stony silence.

Well, here's the good news. At least you were paying enough attention to your audience to notice that your message was not well received. And you also had a clear enough sense of what you wanted from them (laughter, enthusiastic nodding, note taking, questions) to know that you weren't getting it. So, if you'd only been a little flexible, you might have been able to save this ship before it tanked.

Later that afternoon you speak privately with someone who attended your talk. It seems your listeners were under the misconception that the innovations you described might render their jobs obsolete. So when you talked about the Potato Head incident, they felt criticized for past mistakes; while you waxed poetic about the new technology, they were envisioning pink slips; and when you gleefully produced that bar graph, their hearts sank at the thought of all that profit finding its way into pockets other than their own.

Of course, there was no way you could have known all this at the time. Or was there? What if when you first noticed the frowns or the slumping you had put down your text and opened it up for questions, right then and there? Or if you had walked out from behind the podium and voiced your surprise at their strange response to your good news? You probably would have discovered the misunderstanding in a matter of seconds and cleared it up right away by playing a new action: *to reassure*. This minor readjustment could have saved everyone a lot of misery and your presentation would probably have been a big hit. Oh well, better luck next time.

The important point is that you must always respond to what's coming back at you from your listeners. If your actions are helping you achieve your objectives—great, stick with them. If not, be willing to adjust them to get the response you need.

Now, at this point you may find yourself thinking that it's easy to see how all this works when you're actually performing your speech. After all, when you give your presentation you'll presumably have a live audience to bounce off of. But what happens when you're alone in your living room? How can you rehearse interacting when there's no one to interact with?

Well, like any good actor, you'll need to practice the art of conjuring.

Imagining the Audience

From now on, the first step in each rehearsal will be to create imaginary listeners to deliver the speech to. Picture what they look like, what they're doing, how interested they seem. This takes a little practice, of course, but it's not hard, and of all the rehearsal secrets we have to offer, this one's the best.

First, you'll need to decide where your audience is located in the room. It's best to approximate the conditions of the actual presentation as specifically as you can. Are they seated near you or far away? (Use your imagination and turn your office into a vast auditorium if necessary.) Clustered together or spread out? If the group is small, imagine you can connect with each listener individually, and notice how he or she is responding. If the group is large, imagine making significant eye contact with a few people in different parts of the room. Pretend there are real people out there and just allow yourself to get used to what it feels like.

Once you've visualized what the people in your audience look like, deliver your speech, actively imagining how they're receiving everything you say. Does something not sit well with them? Is one of them nodding encouragingly? How do these responses affect you? The idea is to give your imagination free rein at this stage, both to practice different types of audience interaction and to see what different communication behaviors you can find in yourself.

The most important thing to remember when creating your imaginary audience is that they should be *active*. If you're just going to imagine a bunch of duds passively sitting there, you might as well talk to the napping dog. Although audiences often *look* like duds passively sitting there, they're capable of responding to you through body language, vocalizations (laughter, oohs and ahhs, groaning), or sometimes by asking questions, and you should work to elicit favorable responses, even when the people *are* imaginary.

If you feel your communication is not as strong as it could be, shake things up a bit. Try substituting a different set of listeners, like your immediate family, members of the National Rifle Association, your local Girl Scout troop, or whoever. Keep the words of the speech the same, and see what it feels like to say them to a completely different audience. If you can't get excited about telling two hundred mid-level managers about changes in your company's family leave policy, imagine you're talking to a group of working mothers on the front lines who've been fighting for this change for years. Or an audience of senior managers who fear a decrease in productivity and must be convinced of the merits of changing the policy. Whatever you choose, make sure you have a clear reason for speaking to the audience you're imagining. Define your objectives before you begin so you'll know whether you're achieving them over the course of your speech. Experiment with lots of scenarios and note which ones get you most connected to your message and to your audience.

Bill Clinton was said to direct his speeches to the person in the audience who most disagreed with him. Since he didn't actually know who that person was, it was an imaginative exercise, and one that most people would agree worked very well for him. You might find that you, too, like to speak directly to your adversaries. Or, by experimenting with different scenarios, you may discover that the opposite is true for you: You communicate best with people who are on your side. Or maybe your speech went better than ever when you saw your parents in the audience, or when you imagined there was only one person listening to you. The power of the imagination can do wonders for your connection to an audience and help you discover hidden skills at the same time.

Once you've found what gets you pumped up in rehearsal, you can easily transfer these discoveries to actual performance. As every actor knows, the audience can't read your mind. Give yourself permission, therefore, to think whatever thoughts most empower your communication—in rehearsals and when you're on the stage.

The Start–Stop Exercise

No matter how diligent you've been about setting aside rehearsal time, imagining your audience, and choosing objectives, there's no getting around the fact that it's hard to connect with an invisible crowd. Most people begin with the best of intentions but, by the time they've gotten through the first couple of minutes of their speech, they forget all about their imaginary listeners and just start droning through the text. So here's a little exercise that will keep you honest. It's also great for getting your focus off the page, even when you're not very familiar with the words of the script.

The Start–Stop Exercise is basically a run-through of your speech with built-in pauses after everything you say. The idea behind the Start–Stop is to engage fully with your audience after every thought you communicate, to make sure they're receiving your message in the way you intended it. Here's how you make this happen: As you work through your speech, maintain eye contact with your imaginary listeners for an extended (and perhaps uncomfortable) length of time at the end of every sentence or thought. You are not allowed to speak again until you feel you understand exactly *why* the audience needs to hear your next line, based on how they responded to the previous one. Only when you have a strong, clear reason for communicating the next idea can you go on with your speech.

As you can probably tell, the silences in this exercise are every bit as important as the words you say. Since most speakers are uncomfortable with silence, rehearsing your speech this way will feel unnatural at first, but the payoff is worth it. In the words of the great nineteenth-century actor Henry Irving, "It is necessary that the actor learn to think before he speaks." The Start–Stop Exercise will give you the time to do just that.

Of course, when you're rehearsing on your own you'll have to creatively imagine the responses you are getting from the crowd. The more active your imagination, the more animated you're likely to become. Believe it or not, envisioning an audience that's too sympathetic to your cause can sometimes diminish the value of your rehearsal because it leaves you with nothing to fight for. So it helps to mix it up. Simulate conditions where sometimes your listeners are really with you and sometimes they're not. Then you can practice adjusting your message to make it more persuasive.

This is a great exercise to do with a mock audience of friends or colleagues as well as when you're on your own. Because it gets you out of your head and into theirs, it's a potent reminder that you are speaking not for your own benefit but for that of your listeners. No matter how eloquent you think you are, if they don't get it, then it wasn't worth saying. The Start–Stop will also improve your ability to make meaningful eye contact. Instead of simply scanning the room with your eyes, as far too many inexperienced speakers do, you'll get used to using your eye contact to assess listener understanding and promote connection with your audience.

Note: When you execute the Start–Stop Exercise correctly, a five-minute speech could take twenty minutes. Of course it will feel too slow. It's supposed to. Which brings up an important point about the difference between rehearsal and performance: Rehearsal is about process and experimentation, performance is about product and presentation. Just like with your new blue jeans, you should be using rehearsal to stretch yourself and your material in nonhabitual ways, so that when you finally get into performance mode you know the speech inside and out and can wear it naturally and comfortably. Many of the exercises in this book, the Start–Stop included, focus on a particular aspect of the speaking process rather than your finished product. So don't worry if it feels a little out of balance now. Later we'll introduce plenty of exercises designed to help you put it all together.

BELIEVING IN THE SPEECH

As Olivier once told a critic, "An actor persuades himself, first, and through himself, his audience."

From the earliest stages of rehearsal actors are consumed with self-persuasion. Through creative visualization and script exploration, they learn to merge the events in the character's life with their own experiences, convincing themselves of the truth of the playwright's fiction.

Your early speech rehearsals are really no different: If you want your audience to believe in what you're saying, you'll have to learn to believe in it yourself and with your whole heart. This might not be hard if you chose the subject matter of your speech and wrote every word of it; but often your job as a speaker, like that of the actor, will be to make someone else's words, ideas, or agenda your own. So how do you do that?

Julie Harris, famous throughout the world for her portrayal of Emily Dickinson in *The Belle of Amherst,* read about and studied her subject for sixteen years before she ever impersonated her on stage. She even visited Dickinson's house and "went through every room . . . walked where she walked."

Okay, maybe you don't have that kind of time or travel budget. But the principle still holds. You've got to find a way to personally connect with your material—whether through research or imagination. Even if you wrote the speech yourself, you've still got to find a way to *re*connect with the power of the events you are describing, as if you were just now remembering these stories or telling them for the first time. Because for your audience, it *will* be the first time.

Whether you're talking about the time you fell out of a tree when you were eight or the time Marc Antony fell on his sword, there's no point in telling the story unless you communicate an intimate connection to it. One way to create this kind of connection is to spend some time carefully developing a vivid mental picture of the events you are describing, just as an actor would use his imagination to place himself in the world of the play. Close your eyes and try to experience the sights, sounds, even the smells, associated with your story. What did that scraped knee feel like when you fell out of the tree? What color was the bruise? How loudly did people laugh at you? What were you feeling? What do you think the other people in the story were feeling?

The more specific your visualization, the more compelling your remarks will be to the audience. Using the actor's tools of sense memory and emotion recall, you can create an experience that will lift the audience out of their chairs, figuratively speaking, and into the world of your story.

Developing Interest

But what happens if you're not very interested in the stories you're telling, or even the subject matter of your speech? At the risk of stating the obvious: Get interested! If you're bored, even for a moment, you can bet your audience will be too. There are lots of ways to get interested in what you're talking about, from learning more about the facts of your topic, to considering its relationship to the lives of real people, to reading opinions about it that differ from your own. You get to choose your way of looking at it, so choose a perspective that captures your imagination.

Let's say you had to deliver the following passage:

"In 1989, the average number of spatulas in the American household was two; forks, eighteen; spoons, fourteen; and knives, twenty-two; In 1999, the average number of spatulas was one; forks, eighteen; spoons, eighteen; and knives, twenty-two."

It may be hard for you to work up a head of steam over national utensil averages. Sure, you've thought about why they're in the speech and why the audience might need to hear them, but they still seem boring and lifeless. Nonetheless, if this is the speech you are charged with giving, you'd better find a way to get excited about it.

One possibility is to ask yourself what kind of people *might* be interested in these statistics and then to put yourself in their shoes. In fact, this approach, labeled by Stanislavsky as the "Magic If," is one of the core tenets of Method Acting. To help himself believe in the reality of the character's experience, the actor asks, "What might I do if I were really in this situation?" In this way, he not only personalizes the experience but also opens up a world of imaginative possibilities to explore. Similarly, you can ask yourself, "What might I do if the number of utensils per household were really important to me?"

Let's imagine for a moment that you make pancake batter for a living. From this perspective, those statistics seem a whole lot more important. You might wonder, for instance, whether the decrease in spatula use is indicative of a larger trend away from the home-cooked breakfast. Your mind might then move on to contemplate whether the decline in spatulas per household is in any way related to the rise in spoons per household. (Are we consuming more cold cereal and coffee on the run at the expense of the full breakfast?) If you were an economist, you might be interested in the correlation between average per capita income and total number of utensils per household; an environmentalist, in what happened to the spatulas that got thrown away between 1989 and 1999. You get the idea. Using the Magic If to enter the world of someone who has a reason to care might actually make you care a little more yourself.

If you don't feel like going the role-playing route, you can increase your level of interest simply by asking yourself, "What does all this have to do with me?" Is your utensil consumption commensurate with the national averages or does it skew up or down? Why do you think that is? Which is your favorite utensil and why? A little personal context goes a long way toward helping you sell your message to your crowd.

Now ask yourself if there's anything about utensil-per-household statistics that is meaningful to you. If your answer is yes, then you can probably find a way to interest yourself in anything.

Communicating with Enthusiasm

In public speaking as well as in theater, the audience takes its cue from the performer. If you're excited, they'll get excited; if you're indifferent, then they will be too. Now that you've spent some time developing a personal connection to your material, you need to use your rehearsals to practice infusing your listeners with the passion you feel.

According to Meryl Streep, "All an actor has is their heart, really. That's the place you go for inspiration." Oddly enough, many public speakers go out of their way to circumvent the heart, to avoid all emotional expressiveness. They're so afraid of overacting that they don't want to act at all, or they worry that injecting personal feelings into their presentation will somehow undermine their status as "the expert." Quite the opposite is true, however; the more value the material has to you, the more it will have to your audience. By speaking from the heart and sharing your enthusiasm for the subject, you actually increase your expert standing (because only someone who truly knows his stuff would dare to care so much about it) as well as your ability to move the crowd. So, now that you're excited about your material, it's time to share your enthusiasm with your audience.

Some people are naturally enthusiastic communicators. They can make even the most mundane events seem like the stuff of action-adventure movies. Most people are not. If you're someone who can make the latest Arnold Schwarzenegger film sound like a documentary on the digging habits of field mice, don't worry. Like just about every other aspect of public speaking, the habits of enthusiastic communication can be learned.

Here are a few things to try in rehearsal.

APPROACH EVERY SPEECH LIKE A MOTIVATIONAL SPEECH

Take any passage from the speech you've written—the duller, the better! Now, instead of picturing yourself talking to the actual people for whom the speech is intended, imagine you are a college basketball coach, addressing your team moments before the start of a championship game. Use the actual words of your speech but imagine that they are intended to light a fire in this eager but anxious group of young players. Instead of merely imparting information to your team, you need to do what any great coach would do and whip them into a frenzy! If sports aren't your thing, you can imagine you're a preacher firing up a congregation, a politician giving a fervent stump speech, or even Joan of Arc leading the troops into battle. Any situation that requires you to speak from the heart to the heart.

When you've finished, take a moment to consider what effect this visualization had on your communication. Were you more physically active than usual? Were you emphasizing different words than you might have otherwise? Did you care more about the response from your imaginary crowd than you normally would? Any changes you've noted probably have to do with the fact that you were communicating more enthusiastically than you are used to. You might even feel like you were "over the top." But it's important to note that, because you've had years to build up your present communication habits, almost any change in the way you do things might feel like going too far. So you probably aren't as out there as you think.

Now ask yourself, which of these new habits of enthusiastic communication do you think you might successfully incorporate into your actual speech? From now on, any time you feel lethargic about what you're saying, conjure up the coach scenario and let the sparks fly.

GET PHYSICALLY INVOLVED

This one's easy and works every time: Before you begin your speech, do thirty jumping jacks, counting each one out loud as you go. As soon as you get to thirty, jump right in and start your speech. Don't even pause to catch your breath. You may find yourself perspiring or breathing heavily as you speak, and that's just fine. The point is to get your body into a state of excitement and start the speech from there. When your heart is thumping and your physical energy level is high, your vocal energy can't help but follow. Even as your heart and breathing rates return to normal, you'll probably find that your speech retains a quality of urgency that is nonhabitual for you. Try to hang on to this heightened sense of physical involvement all the way through to the end.

The great thing about an exercise like this is that it works with the principles of kinetic memory. With enough practice, your body will start to remember what it feels like to be physically committed while speaking and will automatically return to the heightened energy level it found through the jumping jacks, every time you start your speech.

SAY CHEESE

Here's another psychophysical circuit that can be a great boon to public speakers. As you read this, put a smile on your face. A happy, just-received-great-news kind of smile, twinkling eyes and all. If you keep this up for a few seconds, you'll probably notice a related warm-and-tingly emotional response start to form. Years of smiling in response to positive stimuli creates a channel between the physical action of smiling and the feelings associated with smile-worthy occasions. Seeing others smile can also produce this response (that's why the whole world smiles with you, as the old song goes). What use is this to public speakers? Bright eyes, an open face, an upturned mouth, these are all things we associate with the enthusiastic communicator. They are the outward signs that invite us to share in the speaker's positive experience. Unfortunately, out of nerves, the desire to look professional, or simply unconscious habit, many speakers put on a grim game face as they approach the podium, unwittingly shutting out the audience. To counteract this tendency, take a moment in rehearsal to run through the opening of your speech with a big grin on your face. You'll probably feel foolish. Good. This might make you smile even more. The goofier the better. See what it does to your speech to begin from a grin. Then internalize that smile so you feel it but it's not manifesting itself in an unnatural way, and keep going with your speech. Use your eyes to communicate the smile to your imaginary audience. This is a great way to achieve a warm connection with your crowd, one that looks and feels authentic. Even if you're giving a serious speech, you'll want to find moments to share either an outward or an inward smile, one that lets your listeners know you're with them.

Chapter 5

Mining the Text

"Works that have moved, roused, and astonished successive generations will leave the public cold and even hostile if they do not find proper interpreters."

—SARAH BERNHARDT

THE SPEAKER AS INTERPRETER

Now that you've developed a solid foundation for rehearsing, it's time to turn your attention more specifically to the words you will be saying. Whether you're working from a fully prepared script or simply from notes, your job is to properly interpret your message to the audience, bringing the words to life with clarity and power.

Speeches, like plays, are not meant to be read; they're meant to be performed. It's the live interaction of bodies that gives them their power. Nobody wants to listen to a speaker who seems to be "just reading his script," any more than they want to listen to an actor who seems to be "just reading his lines." Audiences expect more than that. But what exactly is it that they want?

They want to experience a human being meaning what he says, bearing witness to the truth and importance of his words, and caring enough to elicit a response. They want to hear someone *using* words, not just reciting them. They want to know why you're saying the words, what the words mean to you, and what the words should mean to them.

The speech you've written is merely a blueprint for the speech you're going to give. The words themselves will not achieve the objectives of your presentation. Only you can do that.

Page Versus Stage

The role of the speaker is radically different from that of the writer, in part because audiences require different things from the practitioners of each art form. When we read, we work things out for ourselves. When we curl up with a novel, we do all the work of figuring out how the words go together to form sentences; the sentences to form paragraphs; and the paragraphs to form characters, locale, suspense. We put the meaning together. A whole complex experience arises directly from the words on the page.

But your audience will not be reading your script. They'll be listening to it. And listening is an entirely different experience. When we listen—to a speaker, an actor, a conversationalist—we derive a huge portion of the meaning not from the words, but from how the words are said. As most of us can attest, a speech, play, or conversation delivered in monotone can actually manage to convey *less* meaning than we could have gotten from reading the exact same words for ourselves.

When we listen to someone, we expect her commitment to the words she has chosen—as manifested in how the words are spoken—to do much of the work of *interpretation* for us. It's not that we become brainless receptacles, by any means, but we do expect the speaker to clue us in to the value of what she is saying. For example:

When we *read,* we see where paragraphs begin and end; that helps. When we *listen,* we need the speaker to somehow let us know where those paragraph breaks are.

When we *read* "10 percent," we look for clues in the text to help us understand whether that means a lot or a little. When we *hear* "10 percent," we expect clues to come from the tone of voice as well.

When we *read,* we figure out for ourselves how a sentence is related to the one before it and the one after. When we *listen,* the speaker's choice of emphasis must *make* those logical connections clear.

Know What You Mean

Of course, to be able to do all this extra interpreting, the speaker must understand the text at a deep level. Even if you wrote the speech yourself, some more analysis may be required. Do you know why *that particular word* is in *that particular place?* Do you *fully* understand the significance of *every* statistic?

Most people will find that they are aware, perhaps vaguely, perhaps acutely, of problem areas in the text of the speech. Places where the logic doesn't quite hold together. Statements that you yourself don't believe in wholeheartedly. Anecdotes that don't really relate to anything. If you're not quite sure why some part of the speech is there, you have three options:

1. Find out. If someone else wrote the speech, go to that person and ask questions until you understand every aspect of the speech inside out.

2. Decide for yourself. No matter what your involvement so far, as the person who will actually be doing the talking, you are

now the primary creator. You're the one who's going to be on the line, so all the important decisions are up to you. Make up a reason to tell that story. Or to drive that point home. Any reason you can buy into is infinitely better than no reason at all. Remember that the words will not speak for themselves. If you decide to just hope for the best, expect the worst.

3. Change it. If you're not sure why it's there, can't find out why, and can't make up a good reason why, then replace it with something better or get rid of it completely.

Note that the last option is everybody's favorite. Most speakers, upon uncovering a weakness in the text, will go back to the drawing board, trying desperately to find a way to fix the words. That's fine, of course, up to a point. You want the words to be well chosen. But at some point, you have to stop.

COME OUT WITH YOUR HANDS UP!

When a new show is being produced there comes a time when the director will "freeze" the production: There will be no more changes to the script or the blocking or the costumes or anything else. This is necessary because at a certain point in the process everybody needs time to settle into a final version and develop confidence in what they're doing. Actors long for the moment. In fact, Ethel Merman is famous for saying, after receiving one-too-many last-minute rewrites: "Call me Miss Birdseye, fellas. This show's frozen."

The same principle holds true for speeches. Give yourself one more chance to go through the script and fix it up. Do it right now and imagine it's your last chance. Then tell yourself the script is frozen and trust that your oral interpretation will make sense of the words that are currently on the page. Assume these words are exactly right and don't apologize for them, even to yourself.

CONNECTING TO THE WORDS THROUGH SCRIPT ANALYSIS

Now that the text of the speech is in final form, you can actively concentrate on using your oral presentation to bring out all its subtlety and power. Here are some theatrical techniques for enhancing your connection to the words in front of you.

Finding Key Words

Start by going through the script and highlighting crucial words. Which words carry more meaning than others? Which words would necessarily appear in any outline of the speech? Which words have the most punch, emotional value, surprise, or substance? Be on the lookout for strong verbs and colorful nouns. Step back and ask yourself, "What's the point of this sentence?" (from the audience's perspective, of course).

Consider this sentence: "We've found, through extensive research, that the problem affects both youth and adults."

It would not be surprising to hear a speaker say that sentence like this: "*We've* found, through *extensive* research, that the problem affects *both* youth *and* adults." Now, it's unlikely that a succinct outline of this speech would include the words *we've, extensive, both,* and *and*. (In general, you should avoid emphasizing pronouns and conjunctions—they're rarely the meatiest parts of the sentence.) It's more likely that *youth* and *adults* are the important words here, because they seem to indicate the people affected by the problem you're discussing. If that's the case, they should get more emphasis.

Find a way to flag key words in your text to make sure you remember they're important. (Many actors begin their work on a play by "marking the script" in this way.) Underline, use asterisks, highlight, or come up with your own hieroglyphics. As long as you know that the marks mean that a word or phrase has special importance, you're much more likely to emphasize it in a way that makes the meaning and value as clear as possible.

As with many things in this book, there's an art to it. Just getting loud on every underlined word is not going to do it. In the next chapter we'll talk about how you can use pitch, tone, tempo, and body language to produce emphasis. But for now, simply think of your markings as little reminders to your subconscious to keep track of what's important. Only careful, continuous attention to what you're saying and to the response you hope to get from your audience will make your emphasis clear and effective. If you're doing the right kind of thinking, a lot of delivery issues will take care of themselves.

Understanding Echo

"But wait," you say, "I'm pretty smart, and the first way of saying that sentence didn't sound so bad to me." If you had that thought, in some ways you're right. And this points out an important thing to keep in mind as you look for key words: Context is everything.

Let's say some organization other than yours has investigated the problem described in your speech and you've just explained that they did very little research and came to the conclusion that the problem affected neither youth nor adults. In that case, the first delivery given above makes perfect sense: "*We've* found, through *extensive* research, that the problem affects *both* youth *and* adults."

We is emphasized to distinguish from "they"; *extensive* is emphasized to distinguish from how "little" research the other group did; and *both/and* is emphasized to distinguish from the other (incorrect) conclusion of "neither/nor."

This is an example of a common speech pattern that we call *echo*: Words that are repeated (such as *research, youth,* and *adults* in this case) get echoed, or subordinated, and the new material gets emphasized. We do it automatically, and constantly, in everyday conversation. This is both good news and bad. Good, because we're all used to doing it, even though it's probably unconscious, and therefore we should be able to do it pretty easily. Bad, because the fact that everybody does it so naturally means that if you fail to do it when it's called for, you'll sound odd and your meaning may be distorted.

Try this:

Imagine your aunt Millie just said to you, "Jackie went to the store to buy bread." Now respond to her by saying, aloud, as if you were having a simple conversation, "Freddy went to the store to buy milk."

If you really thought about what she said to you and what you were saying to her and why, chances are you replied like this: *"Freddy* went to the store to buy *milk."* The middle part—"went to the store to buy"—was still hanging in the air from when Millie said it to you, so you would have no need to give it special emphasis. If you said, "Freddy went to the *store* to buy milk," anyone listening in would think you hadn't heard her correctly. You emphasize *Freddy* and *milk* because they're the new information, and you echo the rest, vocally subordinating it.

Scour your script for places where words get repeated. Those are probably places where something should be echoed and new information should be highlighted. Practice saying these portions out loud until you feel you have a good grasp of how echo clarifies the meaning. And don't be afraid to go overboard: What feels like overacting usually isn't.

Exploiting Parallel and Oppositional Structure

Echo is a specific example of a larger category of linguistic devices we call parallel and oppositional structure.

Consider this: "In 1995, 76 percent of our members made over a hundred thousand dollars per year. By 1999, 85 percent were pulling in more than three million."

First of all, there's some echo here. The "nineteen ninety" and "percent" are repeated verbatim and should be de-emphasized the second time around. The last *nine* in 1999 should be emphasized, as new and different from the "five" of 1995, and of course the *eighty-five* should be brought out as new and different from "seventy-six."

The slight twist here is that "pulling in more than" should be de-emphasized. Even though those exact words have not been heard yet, the idea is present in "made over" in the sentence before. The more important information is *three million,* which serves the same function in the second sentence as "a hundred thousand" does in the first.

This is an example of a parallel structure, where two parts of an idea are expressed in the same form. The speech was written in this way to point out both similarities and differences in the two pieces of information. It's part of the speaker's job to help the audience understand which pieces of information are being compared to which other pieces.

Just as certain elements of a sentence or paragraph often need to be shown to be performing the same function, sometimes it's important to set elements off against each other:

"I come to *bury* Caesar, not to *praise* him."

Any Marc Antony who came out and said, "I come to *bury* Caesar, not to praise *him*," would be howled off the stage. It makes no sense, because he hasn't carefully figured out which parts of the sentence are in opposition. The sentence is about the difference between burying and praising; and if you don't let us know that you know that, you won't be understood.

Go back through your speech and look for places where parallel or oppositional structures are built into the rhetoric. Do you ever discuss past versus future, new ideas versus traditional wisdom, problems versus solutions, good news versus bad news? Make sure you understand the comparison or contrast, then practice saying those parts out loud, exploiting the structure to maximum effect. You'll probably want to find a simple way of marking your script that helps you remember what to do with these parts.

So far we've been talking a lot about specific words. But don't lose the proverbial forest for the trees. The same concepts hold true for sentences, paragraphs, and even the overall structure of the speech. You've got to know how your ideas relate to one another, what information is new and therefore most important, which concepts are being juxtaposed and whether you want your audience to see them as essentially similar or essentially different. Taking the time to conduct such high-level analysis will strengthen your arguments and help you drive your message home.

CONNECTING TO THE WORDS THROUGH REHEARSAL

As any actor will attest, it's one thing to intellectually grasp the concepts of text analysis and quite another to put them into action. Here are a few exercises that will get you up on your feet saying larger portions of the text out loud, clarifying and powerfully expressing the inherent logic of the speech.

The What? *Exercise*

Get together with a friend who's willing to help you rehearse. Deliver your speech (or at least a good chunk of it) out loud, and ask your friend to listen carefully and say "What?" whenever he thinks you could possibly be clearer or more vivid. Whenever your buddy asks "What?" you repeat the last line until your meaning and intention become clear enough to satisfy him (and to make him stop saying "What?" on that line).

This requires some bravery on the part of the buddy. He should be someone who will be hard on you, daring to ask for clarification frequently and insistently. When you respond, resist the temptation to change the words. Using the exact same words, find a way to make him understand you completely.

Also steer clear of conscious manipulation of inflections:

YOU: "I *went* to the store to buy milk."
BUDDY: *"What?"*
YOU: "I went to *the* store to *buy* milk."

If you think too much about how you're saying it, every sentence will break down into its component parts and cease to have any meaning at all. Much more important than *how* you say a particular word or sentence is *why* you say it. Once you have a clear reason for speaking, you're bound to get your point across. So, instead of trying to change how you say the words, think about the whole thought and concentrate on getting your listener to understand you completely. Again, don't worry about overacting here. Decorum is not the goal; clarity is.

This exercise is designed to counteract the tendency to assume that your meaning is clear if you just get the words out of your mouth. True clarity is clarity of *intent* as well as of literal meaning.

Your listeners need to understand not just what you're saying, but why you're saying it.

In doing the *What?* exercise, you'll probably start to try to pre-empt your buddy by being so clear and vivid that he'll have no grounds for "what"-ing you. When this happens, pay attention to how hard you're working. That's what it feels like to communicate with absolute commitment and clarity. Settle for nothing less.

The Paraphrasing Exercise

A good actor convinces the audience that there is no script—that the character is simply making the words up as he goes along, just as he would in real life. To successfully create this impression, the actor has to "own" the character's words, developing such a deep connection to them that every utterance feels spontaneous and inevitable. The following exercise is designed to help you "own" the words of your speech and increase your connection to the larger meanings of the text.

Now that you've got the words of the speech finalized, throw them away. (Temporarily, of course.) Do the whole thing (or a good chunk of it) without the script, and without even trying to use any of the specific words that are in it. Do it in your own words, off the cuff, impromptu, ex tempore. Just improvise.

The goal is to communicate as much of your message as possible without relying on the preexisting script. Let loose: Say whatever you want. You're free to communicate in your most conversational style, using whatever words come to mind, even going off on tangents if that seems to be a way of getting your overall message across.

Delivering the message of the speech off the top of your head forces you to assimilate the material—to really make it your own—

and also counteracts the all-too-common tendency to view a speech as little more than a list of words that have to get said. Are there whole major ideas you just skipped over? You may have to go back and figure out why those pieces are important. Are there parts that you particularly got into, spending lots of time and getting animated about them? Try to bring that enthusiasm with you when you go back to the script.

In fact, try this: Paraphrase part of the speech and then, without stopping, start up with a random part of the actual text, trying to bring the same animation, "conversational" tone, inflection—everything you had going for you in the improvisation—to the script. Actually imitate the improvisational you. It's a great way to bring life to words that can sometimes look pretty dead on the page.

The Connective Tissue Exercise

Here's another simple exercise to enhance the connection between you and the words. Do part of the speech again, using the exact words of the text, but with a few additions this time. At the end of every sentence, ask a question or provide a transitional phrase. In this example, we've inserted some "connective tissue" into one of the great speeches of the twentieth century:

In the long history of the world, only a few generations have been granted the role of defending freedom in its hour of maximum danger. [*Are we one of those generations?*] I do not shrink from this responsibility—I welcome it. [*Do you?*] I do not believe that any of us would exchange places with any other people or any other generation. [*You're with me on this, I can tell.*] The energy, the faith, the devotion which we bring to this endeavor will light our country and all who serve it—and the glow from that fire can truly light the world. [*Do you see where I'm going with this?*] And so, my fellow Americans, ask not what your country can do for you—ask what you can do for your country. [*You know you'll feel better about yourselves if you do.*]

Try it with your own speech, forcing yourself to add something at the end of every sentence. The idea is to verbalize the subtextual connections from sentence to sentence, to make you more aware of what they are (or might be), and hence more able to communicate them. It should give you a much stronger sense of the sentence-level structure of your speech. If there are places where you can't figure out what to say, study them until you have an idea of an unspoken thought that might go there, then try adding it in.

Once you've done this a couple of times, give the speech again, this time only *thinking* the Connective Tissue transitions without saying the words aloud. Use the thinking pauses to reach out to your audience, making sure they fully understand the logic of your arguments. Keep shrinking the pauses until they disappear altogether, but maintain the connection from thought to thought.

As you can see, this is as much about connecting to your audience as it is about connecting to the words. So now let's turn our attention more specifically to those people who make it all worthwhile.

CONNECTING TO THE AUDIENCE THROUGH THE WORDS

Everyone knows that what you say in a speech matters. But that's only part of the story. How your audience *hears* what you say matters infinitely more. Following are some exercises to make sure that your listeners receive your message in the way you intend.

Good News–Bad News

Take a look at that famous line of Kennedy's: "Ask not what your country can do for you—ask what you can do for your country." Great line, no question about it. Now imagine that instead of Kennedy—the young, vibrant leader inspiring his countrymen to feats of nobility—that speech was given by some bitter, resigned, ineffectual loser of a president (choose a specific name if you like) pitifully begging for help in running the country: "Ask not what your country can do for you—ask what you can do for your country."

How is the inflection different? The use of pitch? What body language would you expect? Everybody will have different answers to those questions, but whatever you specifically imagine, chances are they all translate into one thing for that president's listeners: Bad news.

The point here is that it was very important for JFK to know that he was conveying good news with that line (*If we all pitch in, we can make this country stronger*), and to make sure that his delivery helped him do that.

Pick a sentence or paragraph of your speech at random. Now look at those words. Should they convey good news or bad?

Most people respond to that question by avoiding it. "Neither" is not a good answer. If you decided that what should be conveyed is "neutral news" or "not news at all," you're headed for disaster, or at least a very dull speech. In speaking, no news is bad news.

Your job as a speaker is not only to deliver the facts but also to help your listeners interpret and use those facts. For that reason, news can never be indifferent. Decide what value it has to you and then try to get your listeners to share your sentiments.

To build up some skill in this crucial area, say each of the following sentences twice, once as very good news for your listeners and once as very bad news for your listeners:

2039 will be one of the warmest years in history.

Black is not a color.

I have always depended on the kindness of strangers.

A surprising number of Americans never read a newspaper or watch the news.

The most important advice to bear in mind about the good news–bad news issue is that just about everything you say in your speech must be one or the other. The next most important advice is that most of it should be good.

Of course, at this stage that does not mean going back and changing things in your speech. It just means finding ways of interpreting what you have in positive directions.

Kennedy's speech is a great example of how a really negative situation can be interpreted positively. But pulling that off takes a special act of will. You need to want to be positive. This can be contrary to human nature. Think about this one: "Our organization lost more than seventy-five million dollars last quarter. Next week we'll be having a meeting to discuss what we should do about it. We want everyone to attend."

Most people would probably say that sounds pretty bad. If you stop at your first instinct—that this is all bad news—you stand a decent chance of completely depressing and alienating your audience. Stop and ask yourself: "Why do I need these people to hear this? What do I want them to do?"

Possible answers: "I need these people to hear this so they can share my misery. All I want them to do is feel guilty and suicidal."

First of all, even if you're in such a terrible situation that your answers might really resemble those, be aware that those answers represent only your first and most obvious response. If you try to find something more positive, you will.

How about: "I need these people to hear this because we can't move toward solutions until everyone knows the severity of the situation. What I want them to do is to come to the meeting with some new ideas."

Those answers do not ignore the seriousness of what's going on (there *is* such a thing as bad news), but they also concentrate on why the information is important to the lives of the people in the audience and not just on why the information is important to the speaker. Note that you'll be saying the same words no matter how you answer the questions—the speech is already written—but being on the lookout for every chance to take a positive approach will make a big difference in your delivery and do wonders to keep your audience on your side, where you need them to be.

Lift and Separate

Words and phrases that you've identified as "key" are not the only ones that need special treatment in your delivery. Anything new, unusual, interesting, colorful, or metaphorical needs to be spoken in a way that somehow signals its specialness to the audience. We like to think of emphasizing this kind of thing as "lifting it out" of the text and into the listeners' minds, where they can recognize it as new, unusual, interesting, colorful, metaphorical, or whatever.

Look at that last paragraph. Two expressions are enclosed in quotation marks. Why?

Read the first sentence out loud twice, first ignoring the quotation marks and then thinking of them as integral to the meaning. What do the quotation marks do to your intonation?

There's a good chance that when you say "key" in quotation

marks you slow down a tiny bit as you move into and out of that word. You probably also change your pitch on that word, probably going up a bit. You may also experience a generalized sense of working harder to communicate the specific meaning of that one word, maybe even using your facial muscles more than in the rest of the sentence. You may be tempted to add hand motions to assist the communication. (But no making little quotation marks with your fingers, please.)

Usually the reason words are put in quotation marks is that the person writing the sentence wants to alert the reader that the word is being used in some very specific, perhaps nontraditional way. In the case of the word *key*, the idea relates back to the specific way that word was used in the section "Finding Key Words" on p. 78.

Have another look at the first paragraph of this section. Try the last sentence out loud. Here "lifting it out" is in quotes for a couple of reasons. It's a new phrase, and we wanted to suggest that it is important and will be used later. Also, we're indicating a more metaphorical use of those words than you usually find. We're not lifting something out of the trash here. We're doing something perhaps totally new to you, so this phrase is "lifted out" to signal you that something unusual and potentially interesting is being done with those words.

How does all this relate to your speech? Well, if your script is good, it's probably full of words and phrases that are new, unusual, interesting, colorful, or metaphorical. They probably don't have quotation marks around them, though, and even if they do, your audience won't be able to see them.

If your delivery doesn't convey the intrinsic value of these expressions, your audience will experience a disconnect. They'll wonder: Doesn't he understand that this expression is new, unusual, interesting, colorful, or metaphorical? Or is it actually less special than I think? Of course, both of these responses work against your goals.

Imagine those expressions in quotation marks. (Better yet: Put quotation marks around them.) Lift them out of the text to help your audience recognize how special and interesting they are.

Here's another way to think of the "lifting" idea: Imagine that you're coining certain phrases for the very first time. They've never been used in exactly this way before. Put extra effort into letting your audience know exactly what you mean, because you mean something very specific and you've chosen the perfect word, but without your interpretation, the word itself cannot convey all you have to say.

Your speech probably has a lot more words and phrases that deserve to be lifted out than you will think at first. Have a look at the following sentences and decide what terms should be "set off" from the rest. Each one will probably be set off in a different way— in some cases you may find that quotation marks are not the most suggestive notation to use, so think of the words in bold or italics instead—but each of these sentences would suffer if delivered "straight." Say each sentence aloud, exaggerating the emphasis.

In Part 1, "Getting to Carnegie Hall," we'll discuss the rehearsal habits of several of the century's preeminent musicians.

John Wayne is a figure of mythic proportions.

Perhaps the most important new development is the introduction of Bicoastal Interference Interceptors, or BIIs.

The federal government has been taking a four-year walk on the wild side.

The first one should have been easy, since the quotation marks were already there. But a surprising number of speakers are satisfied to deliver a title like that as though their listeners have known all along what Part 1 was going to be called. They haven't. It's special and interesting and deserving of a tiny extra bit of air time and vocal coloration.

"Mythic proportions" is an exaggeration. Set it off as though you understand that fact, or you're sure to seem pretentious.

A new term like "Bicoastal Interference Interceptors" will often go by too quickly for the audience to really get it. Help them. The same goes for the acronym, because you'll presumably be using it later in the speech and the audience will have to remember it. (This is how you should always introduce acronyms, by the way: directly attached to the full version. Never use an acronym without first saying it in conjunction with the full name unless you are 100 percent certain that everyone in the audience will know exactly what it means.)

And finally, if you're going to use an expression like "walk on the wild side," make sure you're prepared to make fun of yourself just the tiniest bit.

Identifying Beats

Actor Henry Irving had this advice for his fellow thespians: "Remember, first, that every sentence expresses a new thought, and therefore, frequently demands a change of intonation." Good counsel, for public speakers as well as actors. You must know (and help the audience understand) where your thoughts begin and end.

Some speakers are constantly ahead of themselves, on to the next thought before the current one has been fully dealt with. This kind of speaker is known for leaving his listeners in the dust. If you feel you might have a tendency to string sentences together, creating ideas too long for your audience to absorb, you should go back to the Start–Stop Exercise (p. 64). It will force you to identify where thoughts end. It also trains you to use those endings to strengthen your connection with the audience.

The opposite problem is just as common: People who . . . break thoughts up . . . in the middle. Little random pauses can severely interrupt the flow of meaning. This speech pattern can come from using too heavy a hand with emphasis, or from not thinking far enough ahead.

Shakespearean actors, who deal with extremely complicated text, know the value of "thinking the long thought." In other words, they keep the whole thought in mind as they speak each part of the sentence. If you find yourself breaking up the text too often, try thinking (and speaking) all the way to the end of the thought instead of dwelling too much on individual pieces of it. Conversely, if you tend to make long, complex thoughts out of fairly simple ones, try shortening your sense of where thoughts begin and end—just make sure you always think in whole ideas rather than in fragments.

Of course, there are many levels of thought within your speech. There's the sentence level, which we've just dealt with, but there are also higher levels. You need to effectively begin and end each *paragraph*, too, and even each section and subsection of the speech. If you don't, the audience will lose track of how your speech holds together. They'll get lost.

Many actors like to "mark beats" in a script. A beat is a portion of dialogue that seems to be somehow of a piece. That usually means that it's a section throughout which the character is performing the same action (like pleading for mercy). When the action changes (to, say, demanding justice) you have a new beat. To mark the beats is to go through the script and make notations to remind yourself where the beat changes are.

Take another look at your script and place a double slash mark (//) after those sentences that signal the end of a passage or a set of related ideas. This will remind you to pause, breathe, and change your intonation as you move from one beat to the next.

Lists

Another lesson from Shakespeare:

"Hath not a Jew eyes? hath not a Jew hands, organs, dimensions, senses, affections, passions? fed with the same food, hurt with the same weapons, subject to the same diseases, healed by the same means, warmed and cooled by the same winter and summer, as a Christian is?"

Shylock, that famous Merchant of Venice, is driving a point home by reciting a list. A long list, in fact, of the many reasons why Jews should be entitled to the same respect and privileges afforded Christians in Shakespeare's depiction of Venetian society. It's an extremely effective rhetorical device, but only if the actor playing Shylock manages to burn the unique importance of each image contained within the list into the minds of his listeners. If "eyes" sound the same as "hands" and "senses" are indistinguishable from "passions," there's no point in going through every item on the list. Shylock might just as well say "I am the same as you" and be done with it.

Lists are tricky and, like everything else we've covered, require a little extra oomph in the delivery. Throughout the recitation of any list, you need to make sure your audience understands two things: (1) that they're listening to a list and (2) what's in the list. (And that's not as easy as it sounds.)

To achieve number one, begin by asking yourself, "What unites the items in this list?" Are they steps in a procedure, important concepts to be addressed later in the speech, positive trends? For your audience to appreciate the internal unity of the list, you need to keep that unity in mind as you deliver it. There also has to be something similar about how each element of the list is said. Maybe it's a slight upward inflection at the end of each element to carry you on to the next. Maybe it's small pauses before and after each element. An unaccounted-for *change* in the inflection pattern in the middle of a list may seem to signal the beginning of a new sentence, which disrupts the meaning.

The next step is to ask: "How is each of these things special or unique?" Do the elements of the list increase in importance, drama, absurdity? Making each new thing somehow better than the one that comes before it is a wonderful way to give shape to a list and keep your audience engaged.

Sometimes you don't need the audience to understand much more than the fact that the list is long. "The kitchen counter was overflowing: Bread, milk, artichokes, tomatoes, cereal, potatoes, chicken thighs . . ." If the main point is that there was a lot of stuff on the counter, you can afford to move very quickly through the list.

Sometimes lists contain information that is wholly new to your listeners or crucial ideas that need to be remembered. "The steps of cardiopulmonary resuscitation (CPR) are (1) call 911, (2) check breathing, (3) give two breaths, (4) check pulse, (5) position hands, (6) pump fifteen times." Here it's about the individual things in the list as much as it is about the list itself, and you'll need to take your time to make sure your listeners get every point. Knowing which kind of list you're presenting will help keep your audience understanding you in the way you want them to.

Statistics

Is 83 percent high or low?

Well, if it's the percentage of murders that go unsolved in a major U.S. city, most people are going to consider it high. If it's a high schooler's algebra average and she had a 96 percent last semester, then it's low.

Statistics have no meaning without interpretation. Once again, if we're reading, we search for clues in the context to help us understand how to do the interpreting. If we're listening to you, we need you to use your voice to interpret for us.

How do you do that? As with so many things, it's best to use your intuition (along with a good sense of the range of expression you are capable of—see chapter 6). Without thinking too much, try each of these examples out loud. Decide on an interpretation (big or small?) for each statistic, then do everything you can to strongly communicate that interpretation:

Last year, 83 percent of our income came from contributions. This year the figure was 91 percent.

In the class of '27, forty kids went on to college. There were forty-two high school seniors in the whole town.

Reducing our national garbage output to five million tons per year is a physical impossibility. Five million tons of garbage are thrown into Marina Bay every month.

If you found yourself working harder at communicating the value of those numbers than you ever would have thought necessary, good. If not, go back and try them again. It may feel like overacting, but it's the only way to make numbers come alive for your audience. If you fail to do it, you may succeed in obliterating the value of every statistic in your speech.

You may have noticed that this whole idea is intimately tied to that of good news–bad news. Both are about helping your audience see the information the way you want them to see it. They will only be able to do that if they are absolutely clear about how you see it. So don't be afraid to let them know. Go ahead and be a little dramatic about it.

SPECIAL DELIVERY

Telling Stories

The art of telling stories may be the public speaking skill that is closest to the art of acting. In an anecdote there is no way to escape the need to *personalize* the material. The audience will only appreciate the value of your story if they understand its value to you.

In the last chapter you spent some time connecting to the emotional and physical specifics of the stories you're telling. Now it's time to think about how best to communicate those specifics to your listeners.

Use your stories to actively reach out to your audience. As you are sharing your experience (or your personal interpretation of someone else's experience), imagine that your unspoken subtext is, "I know we've *all* experienced something like this . . ." That's a great way to create a sense of intimacy with your listeners and to keep them constantly engaged on a personal level, which is of course the only level that ever really counts.

Great storytelling requires you to keep both the details and the overall value of each story in mind as you tell it. Help the audience understand how one event relates to another in the story, where the events build to a climax, and what the ultimate lessons are. Most important, your stories *must* connect in some way to the substance of the speech. The connection can be peripheral, but don't let yourself simply go off on a tangent without giving the audience a good reason why you just lengthened a speech that they may already think is too long. Your speech should already make or imply the connection, but be sure—before, during, and after your story—that you're well aware of how your story relates to your point. Keeping that connection uppermost in your mind will help you make the relevance clear to your audience.

Using Humor

If you consider yourself the life of every party, congratulations. But remember, you don't have to be a funny person to use humor effectively in a speech. Broadway acting coach Fred Silver once noted that Nancy Walker, one of the greatest comediennes he'd ever worked with, was also one of the most serious people he had ever met. So take heart: Even if you think you're about as funny as a crutch, your habitual social persona should prove no barrier to using humor in a speech.

Of course, that's not to say that your personality doesn't come into play at all. If you've never been able to tell a joke well, then jokes might not be the best form of humor for you to use. If you were in on the writing of your speech, we've already advised you to do some thinking about what kind of humor suits you (see page 42).

Quite often, the best opportunities for humor in a speech come from lines that might not seem funny on the surface, but have hidden potential for creating irony or getting the audience to identify with life's little absurdities.

Let's now turn our attention to the group of teachers known among the students as the Lords of Discipline.

Many members of the council seem to think this problem will just disappear.

Now, that first one might strike you funny, might not. If it does, great. Exploit the humor you find there. If it doesn't, *find* the humor. Create it. We're not talking hilarity here. Just a quiet awareness, a moment of levity.

The first sentence on page 98 could be delivered straight, in utter seriousness. How much better, though, to lift "Lords of Discipline" in a way that shows you understand this to be a somewhat silly description. Invite the audience to smile inwardly at the cleverness of the students, or at the excessive disciplinary enthusiasm of this group of educators. Let them know you share their interpretation. Be in on the joke, however small it may be.

A straight delivery of a line like that is not necessarily a problem unless a lot of audience members see humor where you fail to find it, which may make you seem a bit of a stick in the mud.) You just want to make sure you seize every opportunity to reinforce the audience's feeling that you're with them, on their side, in their camp.

How about that second example? Nothing immediately humorous there. But try making the slightest good-natured fun of the council by literalizing the metaphor. Imagine they think the problem will actually, truly, magically *disappear* from view. Put the last word of the sentence in quotation marks or italics and use it to nudge the council (a little or a lot, depending on what you think is safe and appropriate). Try it out loud and see what happens to your delivery. The idea is to communicate that you know that many in the audience would like to see that council ribbed a little, so you're just obliging them.

Of course, both these examples might be handled entirely differently depending on the context. If the problems were deadly serious, a completely straight delivery might be best. But the general principle is to look for as many chances for lightness as you can find.

Now let's say you have a real joke in the script. It may take a little extra rehearsal to get to the point where you feel completely comfortable telling it. Most actors will tell you that comedy is harder than tragedy any day.

First of all, never apologize for a joke in any way. No "Stop me if you've heard this one" or "Indulge me for just a moment." No shrugging or other apologetic body language. If the joke is in the speech, you should already have determined that it's appropriate, relevant to the material, and worth telling. (See p. 42 for advice on how to choose humorous material.) Don't let self-consciousness undermine the humor, because you can trust that it will.

If you think the joke is just the stupidest thing you've ever heard and can barely bring yourself to tell it, but you know you have to for one reason or another, try this: Think of somebody you know who finds this kind of joke funny. (You probably can think of somebody if you try—remember, respecting that person's sense of humor is not required.) Then tell the joke as if you were speaking directly to that person, the person who is most likely to enjoy it. That can help a lot.

If you're worried that the problem is not with the joke itself but with your ability to tell it well, there are a couple things you can do to help yourself. Memorize it, for one. Even if you haven't memorized the rest of the speech, always be prepared to do humorous sections from memory. Humor is about creating an especially intimate relationship with your audience, and you can't do that if you're glued to the page.

As with any story, spend some time personalizing your connection to the joke. Visualize a time when you found yourself in some similar (though maybe less ridiculous) situation. You don't need to "act out" the different roles in the joke, but you should have some sense of what those poor characters are going through.

It's important, also, to make sure you understand the logic of the joke. Almost every joke has a punch line—be sure you know where it is. How does the joke build to the punch line? Is it a classic three-parter? (Help us know when each part begins and ends.) Does the humor come from a last-minute reversal of expectations? (Do your best to lead the audience down the wrong path.)

The punch line needs to stand out, and it must be given time to land before you move on to whatever comes next. This is the most dangerous moment in telling a joke. Most people are so worried about getting the laugh that the instant just after the punch line is fraught with tension: They didn't get it. They don't think it's funny. I'm a big idiot.

This is a crucial place to practice the Start–Stop technique. When you reach the end of the punch line, stop. Don't start again until you've shared a nonverbal moment with the audience in which you silently communicate the value and humor of what you've just offered them, *even if they're not laughing*. Even if they're scowling. The lack of a laugh doesn't mean the joke has failed; every joke does something different to every audience, and some audiences are more demonstrative than others. *Assume* (or, if you're of a pessimistic bent, *pretend*) that the joke went over great, and refuse to rush out of it like it's a burning building. Sometimes audiences fail to respond to jokes they actually thought were funny because the speaker hasn't given them time or permission to laugh. Be courageous. Take the time and get the pay-off you deserve.

Of course, the audience's response to your joke will probably be perfectly pleasant (something between the uproarious guffaw you're hoping for and the cricket sound you're fearing). If you dare to tell the joke as though it's funny, it usually will be.

REHEARSAL CHECKPOINT

Now that you've identified key words and phrases; plumbed the script's echoes and parallel and oppositional structures; tried the *What?*, Paraphrasing, and Connective Tissue Exercises; explored good news–bad news; rehearsed lifting; worked on clearly beginning and ending your thoughts; clarified your lists; vivified your statistics; personalized your stories; and enlivened your speech with humor, it's time to put it all together. Pick up your freshly marked script, decide who you are talking to, and deliver it—with all the power, clarity, and value you possibly can.

When you've finished, jot down a few notes about how you think it went. Were you as forceful as you had hoped to be? Were you getting your words off the page and into the minds of your imaginary listeners? Did you remember to let your ideas land? Developing new habits is hard work and it's important to celebrate your progress as you move through the training in this book. When you've analyzed your performance and given yourself a healthy round of applause, you're ready to move on to the next step: developing effective body language and mastering vocal technique.

Chapter 6

Centered Communication

"Suit the action to the word, the word to the action."
—WILLIAM SHAKESPEARE, *Hamlet*

THE BODY AND THE VOICE. THEY ARE THE ACTOR'S INstruments, the physical tools that turn theatrical ideas into dramatic action. With so much riding on the ability to communicate through so few tools, it's no wonder that actors spend years learning to tune their instruments, developing the physical and vocal technique that will enable them to captivate an audience in role after role.

Public speakers, on the other hand, tend to forget that speaking is as much a physical activity as a mental one. More often than not they skip the physical and vocal preparation and simply try to *think* themselves into a performance-ready state.

But as with acting, powerful public speaking requires the speaker to be in absolute control of the physical as well as the psychological aspects of communication. It's a state of performance readiness actors call "being centered," when all of you is available for the task at hand.

This chapter provides practice in the skills of powerful, centered physical and verbal communication. You'll be introduced to the basic elements of the actor's technique and learn to use the unique aspects of your own physical and vocal presence to command the attention of the room and control the image you project behind the podium.

PHYSICAL COMMUNICATION

A lot of speakers feel pretty good from the neck up. It's the rest of the body that's the problem: legs that twitch indiscriminately, hips that swivel inappropriately, hands with minds of their own.

Ever since the early 1970s, when Julius Fast made the idea famous in his book *Body Language,* everyone has been aware that what you do with your body—how you sit, stand, smile, or cross your legs—speaks volumes about who you are and how you feel.

Since everything you do says something, it's important to remember what you want to say. Keeping in mind what message you're trying to convey is much more important than memorizing lists of body language do's and don'ts.

When an actor feels really in touch with a role and what's happening onstage, he is rarely aware of exactly how his body is behaving. If you asked him after the show to tell you what he did with his hands, he probably wouldn't be able to. That's because he was "in the moment," concentrating on the character's needs and interactions. His movements happened naturally, because they served the purposes of the character at the time.

This is the state you want to achieve. The ubiquitous lists of do's and don'ts usually just frustrate people and make them self-conscious—in other words, they do the exact opposite of what they should do. When you're fully engaged in communicating with your audience, much of how your body is behaving should just take care of itself.

Unfortunately, this relaxed, engaged, centered state doesn't always come naturally. But it's possible to cultivate it. You begin by examining your habits of physical communication to determine which ones are working for you and which ones are working against you.

Bad Habits

We may be constantly trying to kick 'em or break 'em, but we all have habits, and lots of them. They are the actions we repeatedly perform, sometimes consciously, often unconsciously. Some habits grease the wheels of social interaction and help us get along in the world, like saying "excuse me" when you bump into a stranger on the subway; others accomplish little, like biting your nails. For every seven highly effective habits, there are eight more that won't get you anywhere.

Sarah Bernhardt said, "If you would be natural, you must avoid the persistent mannerisms that actors frequently adopt, believing they please the public. In the end, these become merely bad habits." Though she he was referring to the histrionic mannerisms employed by actors of her time—like grand arm gestures, exaggerated facial expressions, and oh-so-rounded vocal tones—she might just as well have been addressing modern-day speakers. Very often, developing effective technique as a public speaker isn't so much a matter of learning new habits as unlearning old ones. Once you divest yourself of the mannerisms that work against clarity of communication, you can feel what it's like to speak and move naturally and spontaneously.

Take a look at your public speaking style. Think back to a recent speech you gave or take a moment to deliver (as if you were doing it for real) the opening passage of the speech you are currently working on. Is your body working for you or against you?

It's working for you if your public speaking style resembles the best of your private speaking style—but on a slightly enlarged scale. That means a close friend could walk into the room while you're rehearsing and immediately feel like he was seeing the real you—that is, the real you when you're talking passionately about something really exciting or important. If it seems as if someone else were up there, an unusually uptight version of your real self or an overly mannered impostor, it's time to start kicking the habits that are getting in your way.

The best way to analyze your use of the body and voice is by watching yourself on videotape. If you have access to a camera, tape a five-minute portion of your speech. Be aware that everyone hates the way they look on tape, and try not to judge yourself too harshly. But look closely and try to identify which qualities and habits are helping and which are hindering you. If you can't record yourself, get a trusted friend to watch you. Ask for honest, specific feedback about your voice and physical presence.

Directed Movement

In his famous advice to the traveling players, Prince Hamlet cautioned, "Nor do not saw the air with your hand, thus, but use all gently." It's easy to guess what Hamlet meant by *thus:* hands that, by the sheer magnitude of their activity, seem to be doing a lot of talking, but in fact have nothing to say.

Any movement that comes across as a personal habit rather than a purposeful gesture loses all meaning. And random use of the hands is one of the most insidious of the meaningless habits that plague both actors and public speakers.

The first step in dealing with the issue of hyperactive hands during performance is to develop an awareness of when you are gesturing with them and why. Try this experiment: Take a passage from your speech and go way overboard with your hands as you deliver it, gesturing on every line or even every word. Then do it again, moving your hands only when you feel you absolutely must to make something clear. Once more, not moving your hands at all. Finally, take the passage one more time and let your hands move whenever and however they want.

Exploring the extremes will help you develop a sense of how much is too much. Keep concentrating on the hand issue in isolation, until you feel comfortable allowing them to relax in a neutral position (on the podium, at your sides, even in your pockets occasionally) until they are called to action for a purposeful gesture, like pointing to an object, demonstrating the largeness or smallness of something, or shrugging at the sheer inexplicability of it all. After a little practice, you'll be able to shift your focus back to communicating your message to the audience, and your hands will naturally know what to do.

Randomness of movement can affect the feet, as well. Many presenters shift their weight from foot to foot while they are speaking, often without even realizing they're doing it. It's a habit that suggests the speaker is dissipating energy rather than harnessing it, and audiences will usually find the shuffling distracting. Use your rehearsals to practice comfortably standing still with your feet firmly planted on the ground.

If you discover that there are times when you repeatedly fall prey to weight shifting, you may have excess energy that needs a proper outlet. Instead of rocking from side to side, try making a strong, directed move—like walking out from behind the podium to tell a particularly intimate story or crossing the stage to more actively engage listeners on the far side of the room.

Freedom of Movement

While some speakers suffer from doing too much with their bodies, others have the opposite problem. Hamlet offers some guidance here, too. He advised the players: "Be not too tame neither, but let your own discretion be your tutor."

In other words, trust that it's okay to move. In fact, it can be a great attention focuser for your audience—as long as you move with purpose. If you're inclined to cling tight to the podium, force yourself in rehearsals to go too far in the other direction. You'll never learn how to break out of the small box you've put yourself in until you experience the opposite. Walk around. Pretend you're Oprah Winfrey going out into the audience to make one-on-one contact with the crowd. Or imagine you're a fire-and-brimstone preacher revving up your audience with high-energy gesticulation. Don't worry about being over the top. You can always pull back later. By allowing yourself to use your body in nonhabitual ways, you'll experience what it's like to be physically free and unafraid of making a mistake. Actors call this freedom to move without self-consciousness "being in your body." Speakers who manifest it never fail to win the confidence of their listeners.

Posture

Actors devote a lot of attention to developing a posture that is "straight-up," which means standing tall, feet firmly planted on the ground, head floating comfortably atop a fully aligned spine. That's because people associate straight-up posture with winners. Slouching is for losers. Look at the way Jason Alexander played George Costanza on *Seinfeld*. Hunched shoulders, spine collapsed at waist, weight shifting aimlessly from foot to foot. Telltale signs that this character is a low-status player in the world. Now think of Denzel Washington in *Glory, Malcolm X,* or just about any role he's ever played. His spine is straight, his bearing almost regal. Whether he's a slave, a prince, or the leader of a revolutionary movement, Washington projects something noble, a person whose influence goes beyond his station in life. If you want people to see you as someone whose authority they should respect, posture is key.

Here's a quick and easy way to experience an authoritative yet comfortable posture: With your feet shoulder-width apart, go up on your tiptoes and hold there for a count of three. Then, keeping the top of your head where it is, slowly bring your heels back to the floor. (We know this isn't strictly possible, but take an actorly leap of the imagination and give it a try!) Now take a deep breath, and relax your neck and shoulders on the exhale.

What you're experiencing now is what it feels like to stand comfortably straight-up, a powerful position for any speaker. Keep this posture and run through a passage of your speech, using your new-found height to empower you.

Facial Expressions

Most speakers aren't aware of how often their brows furrow and their lips purse even when they're delivering the most heartfelt and enthusiastic of messages. As Juliet tells her nurse, "Thou shamest the music of sweet news by playing it to me with so sour a face."

The key to developing purposeful expressiveness is simply to make sure what you are doing with the muscles in your face matches your words, tone, and overall point of view about your message at any particular moment. This doesn't mean layering on a phony smile or widening your eyes in mock surprise or doing anything else that feels inauthentic. More often than not it means removing the unconscious impediments that short-circuit your natural ability to communicate expressively.

Take another look at the videotape you've made, or solicit a friend's opinion. If you find that your expression seems "closed off" when you're communicating something positive, try consciously raising your eyebrows while you rehearse. This simple adjustment makes a world of difference, giving the (presumably accurate) impression that you are empathetic and open rather than emphatic and stern.

If you have the opposite problem—maybe you've got an inappropriate smile on your face or a Groucho Marx thing going on with your eyebrows even when you're delivering bad news—you need to learn to relax the muscles in your face. The next time you rehearse, imagine that you have awakened from a deep sleep just moments before you start speaking. You won't have any extra energy to waste on excessive facial movements. Just focus on getting your message across as clearly and directly as possible. You may notice that your features seem to soften when you do this exercise, a clear sign of the release of facial tension.

The Eyes Have It

If you've been working with the Start–Stop Exercise (p. 64), you should by now be familiar with the all-important role of eye contact in bringing your words to life for your audience. This probably wasn't news to you. Everything you'll ever hear about public speaking will tell you to look them in the eye.

But for all the lip service given to it, eye contact is too often equated with keeping your head up and periodically scanning the audience. True eye *contact,* however, requires that you achieve a *connection* with the eyes you meet. It tells the audience you're paying attention to them and care what they think. Any actor who fails to make this kind of meaningful connection with the other actors in a play or movie quickly becomes box office poison, and a public speaker who fails to make it with an audience runs the risk of becoming a self-absorbed drone.

The goal of eye contact is intimate involvement. Each time you look at someone, you are having a brief conversation with that person, an exchange of thoughts and feelings. Because your audience members may not have any lines in your "scene," the only way they get to communicate with you is through their eyes. So you need to listen to what they are telling you.

Good speakers are other-oriented, meaning they care more about what's going on with their listeners than what's going on with themselves. A difficult task when, let's face it, you're the center of attention. Learning to truly listen and reflect back what your eyes are "hearing," however, will not only make you a better speaker but will also alleviate the self-consciousness that can come from the misconception that you're entirely on your own up there.

The Mirror

Actors have a great training tool they use to help them get out of their heads and into the minds of their scene partners. It's known as the Mirror Exercise and it's a wonderful way to increase your sensitivity to the needs of your audience. Here's how you can make it work for you.

Enlist the help of an open-minded friend and sit down opposite each other, either on the floor or in chairs. Now adjust your positions so that you are mirror images of each other. Make sure the position is comfortable for both of you and just relax into it, allowing yourself to eliminate all extraneous motion.

The next step is the most crucial aspect of the exercise: Establish eye contact with the other person and don't let yourself break it for the duration of the exercise. It may be uncomfortable at first, but the act of will that it requires is absolutely essential.

From this point on, everything the two of you do should be done as if in a mirror. If one of you needs to scratch an itch, you both must do the movement at the same time and in exactly the same way. This requires that all movements be in extreme slow motion.

Once you've established eye contact, your friend should begin an abstract slow-motion movement, being sure to keep it slower and smoother even than seems necessary. Without breaking the eye contact, follow her movements exactly. See if you can even mirror the "spirit" of what's coming at you. Giggling is allowed, but it must be mirrored. Ideally, someone walking into the room should not be able to tell who's initiating the movement.

After about five minutes of this, you can take over the lead of the movement. Just remember to keep it slow and smooth so that your partner can follow it exactly. At the end of another five minutes, break the mirror and discuss the following questions:

Did you find it easy to maintain the eye contact? Why or why not?

Did you prefer following or leading? Why?

What level of success do you think you achieved in staying together?

What was your level of self-consciousness?

Did the exercise get easier as it progressed?

This is great exercise to repeat, either right now or any other time when you can find a willing accomplice.

As you've probably surmised, the Mirror Exercise is a training tool rather than a model for how you should relate to your audience during your speech. To suddenly start mirroring the movements of your crowd would be odd, to say the least. But a little experience with the mirror will show you how far you can go in connecting to another person, how aware you can be of their unspoken thoughts, questions, and needs. Once you've dared to get this intimate with your mirror partner, relating to your audience in an open, empathetic, and responsive manner should be a whole lot easier.

VERBAL COMMUNICATION

Asked about the experience of preparing to play Othello, Sir Laurence Olivier confessed, "I didn't think I had the voice for it." A surprising sentiment from an actor universally acclaimed for the richness and resonance of his vocal tones. And proof that even the most gifted performers experience insecurity when it comes to the way they sound.

"I hate my voice" is a common refrain from public speakers, and a sad one. Your voice is as much a part of who you are as how you look or what you feel or the way you think. It's an expression of your individuality—formed not only by the luck of the biological draw but also through years of responding to your particular social environment. In fact, our voices are so closely tied to our uniqueness as human beings that voice prints are reliably used as a means of identification, just like fingerprints.

A part of your job as an effective speaker is to make peace with your vocal instrument. If you're someone who's all too aware of real or imagined shortcomings in your own voice, don't despair. Vocal habits are as easy to address as physical ones; all it takes is a little purposeful self-examination and the willingness to practice the habits of effective, confident verbal communication.

Lending Your Ears

To accurately assess your oral presentation, you need to hear yourself the way others do. In the following exercise, you'll play both the communicator and the receiver of the communication at the same time.

Deliver a five-minute portion of your speech to a tape recorder, just as you would hope to deliver it to an audience. Next, listen to the recording you made of yourself. Imagine that someone you don't know is doing the talking, and simply hear what that person has to say.

When you've finished listening, write down your responses to the following questions, playing back portions of the tape if necessary:

What part of the tape sounded best to you? Why?

What part seemed most important to the speaker? Why?

What was the main point the speaker was making?

Were you persuaded to agree with the speaker's point of view? Why or why not?

Were there parts you didn't understand? If so, what seemed to be getting in the way?

Which of the following adjectives honestly seem to apply to this speaker?

Logical	Enthusiastic	Energetic	Committed
Authoritative	Bored	Boring	Lively
Shy	Powerful	Friendly	Insincere
Intelligent	Incoherent	Sincere	Patronizing
Monotonous	Charismatic	Stiff	Direct

If you answered all of these questions exactly the way you would hope to have an audience member answer them about you, then you can skip the rest of this exercise.

Otherwise, look over your answers once again and decide what aspects of your vocal communication you would like to improve.

Now, there's a big danger in trying to correct vocal problems. The danger is that your speech will end up becoming stilted and unnatural because you're trying to follow too many rules.

Remember, one rule takes precedence above all: *Always speak for the benefit of your listeners.* Even as you attend to the specifics of your vocal presentation, don't lose sight of the need to reach the audience with your message and achieve the overall objectives of your speech. With that caveat in mind, here are some suggestions for addressing common vocal difficulties you may be experiencing.

Voice Complaints Here

LACK OF PROJECTION

Powerful messages demand powerful delivery. Which means you must make sure you are heard, understood, and believed by every listener in the room. The speaker who lacks the ability to project has a hard time making his audience sit up and pay attention.

Simply increasing your volume will physically assert your presence right from the top and command the attention of the room. It will also get you more involved with what you're saying and probably even reduce your nerves, because when you act powerful you feel powerful. Even when you're speaking with a microphone, you need to keep up your vocal energy. If you're worried about being too loud, turn the microphone down a notch and let your real voice do the heavy lifting.

If projection is a problem for you, try this imaginative adjustment: Instead of picturing yourself in your living room or a medium-size conference room or even the real hall in which you'll be speaking, imagine you're delivering your speech in a Greek amphitheater. (Remember, they didn't have microphones back then.) Make sure your message is energetic enough to reach the ears of even the farthest plebeian.

Most people feel they're talking really loudly when they're not (everything sounds different from inside your own head). So get used to pumping up the volume beyond what seems natural at first.

POOR BREATH CONTROL

Simple adjustments in breathing—moving from shallow chest breathing to deep diaphragmatic breathing—can produce remarkable improvements in all aspects of vocal communication, including increasing your volume and helping you sustain your energy over the course of a long speech.

Most novice speakers don't breathe often enough during performance. They're afraid of taking up the audience's time with their own physiological needs, or they simply forget to breathe, out of nervousness. Audiences know that the speaker is a human being, with normal human needs, so don't be shy about coming up for air when you need to.

When you do stop for a breath, make sure it's a productive one, meaning it originates in your diaphragm (the muscle in your abdomen that expands and contracts as you breathe), not in your chest. If you've never consciously experienced deep, diaphragmatic breathing, try the following exercise.

Take a deep breath in and exhale fully. Note what happens on the inhale. If your stomach contracts or your shoulders rise, you're a victim of the military style, suck-in-your-gut kind of shallow breathing. It's an ineffective way of taking in oxygen and tends to cause more tension than it releases. Try it again, this time placing your hand on your stomach. Allow your abdomen to expand as you fill up with air and contract as you release the air. Your shoulders shouldn't need to move at all.

Stomach expansion on the inhale and contraction on the exhale is a sure sign that you're breathing efficiently and with your diaphragm. Even though this is the most natural way of taking a breath—it's how we breathe when we're asleep—many of us have been socially conditioned to do the opposite. As a result, you may have to consciously practice this method until it becomes second nature for you. Once you've mastered the deep breathing technique you'll soon find yourself able to speak more energetically over a longer period of time.

DOWNWARD INFLECTION PATTERN

Downward inflection pattern (DWIP for short) is the tendency to let the energy of a sentence drop off at the end. If your sentences start off strong but lose volume and clarity before the thought is completed, you, like millions of other Americans, are a DWIP sufferer.

Listen to your audiotape again. If you notice any DWIP, read the speech passage into the tape recorder again and this time concentrate on making the very last word in each sentence the most important one. Newscasters use this technique all the time to keep audiences from tuning out between stories. It's a great trick for maintaining energy throughout a whole thought. And it counteracts the worst effect of DWIP: the feeling that the speaker is not particularly interested in what he's saying.

Emphasizing the last word will feel artificial at first, but remember, it's only an exercise. The point is to get used to caring that your listeners receive the complete value of what you have to say. Simply being aware of DWIP tendencies usually makes a big difference in a person's vocal self-presentation.

UPWARD INFLECTION PATTERN

As you may have guessed, upward inflection pattern (UWIP) is the flip side of DWIP. It means your pitch rises at the end of every sentence, making even the strongest statements into questions? You can see how jarring it is?

UWIP is a speech pattern that suggests uncertainty and the need for affirmation, as if the speaker is asking for the audience's approval. ("Did you get that? Do you know what I mean?") It's a particularly insidious habit of gen Xers, although it's becoming more and more common to hear it across corporate America. As you might imagine, UWIP undercuts authority and undermines the credibility of the speaker. If you heard yourself manifesting symptoms of UWIP as you listened to your tape, try the speech again, this time making sure you deliver your statements as statements— strong, definitive assertions. If there are times in your speech when you feel a statement calls for some kind of affirmation from the audience, that's fine. Deliver your statement full force, then follow up with a question. "Petty crime is on the rise in our neighborhood. Has this been your personal experience?" There's nothing wrong with asking questions as long as that's what you intend to do. It's the wishy-washiness of unintended questions that you want to avoid.

Speaking Too Fast or Poor Articulation

If your words go by too quickly, your audience will not have a chance to understand their full value. The same goes for mumbling. And, of course, making your listeners understand the full value of your words is your primary concern.

If you have either of these problems, here's a great imaginative exercise that will help. Imagine that your listeners are very intelligent but not very fluent with the English language. You don't want to sound patronizing, but you need to make sure they understand every word. Try it with your tape recorder and see if it makes a difference.

You can also practice the habits of clear, precise articulation by using tongue twisters. An old actor's favorite, heard in dressing rooms around the country, is "red leather, yellow leather." Repeat this phrase twenty times (breathing whenever you need to), accelerating a little each time you say it. Concentrate on really getting your mouth around those words and overarticulating the consonants. If you train your articulation muscles to be a little more active than they are habitually, you'll find that everything you say becomes a little easier. This is also a great exercise to do with one of the actual phrases from your speech. Pick something you always stumble over and treat it like a tongue twister. Exaggerate the sounds as you say them, and accelerate your delivery with each repetition.

Stilted Delivery

If you sounded more stiff or formal on the tape than you would like, you probably need to adopt a simpler, more conversational style. Follow Aristotle's advice and "Think as wise men do, but speak as the common people do." Try using more contractions and splitting your infinitives, just like you would if you were talking around the dinner table. Keep your sentences short and the logic clear.

Imagine that you're speaking to a close friend—someone you don't need to impress. Tape yourself again with this in mind and you'll probably hear a marked difference in the intimacy and casualness of your tone.

MONOTONOUS OR METRONOMIC DELIVERY

If your voice sounded flat or boring even though you felt excited about what you were saying, you might be underusing the tools of pitch and tempo variation. Pitch, of course, refers to the highness or lowness of your vocal tones; tempo is how quickly or slowly you utter your words. As you discovered in chapter 4, a change in pitch is a great way to draw the audience's attention to a key word or new idea. Similarly, a change in the pace of your delivery can help the audience feel when your speech is headed toward a climax or when you are leading them through a particularly complicated idea. If you're not used to thinking about these issues, try a little experiment.

Read aloud the following passage, from a speech by John F. Kennedy:

> I see little of more importance to the future of our country and our civilization than the full recognition of the place of the artist. If art is to nourish the roots of our culture, society must set the artist free to follow his vision wherever it takes him.
>
> In a free society, art is not a weapon and it does not belong to the sphere of polemics or ideology. Artists are not engineers of the soul. . . .
>
> The highest duty of the writer, the composer, the artist is to remain true to himself and to let the chips fall where they may.

Now underline twenty words that you think are important in this passage and read it aloud again, highlighting those words through changes in pitch. Since many speakers have difficulty distinguishing between changes in pitch and changes in volume, you should tape yourself to ensure that you have truly accomplished pitch variety (meaning you actually hit different notes on the musical scale as you emphasize key words). Once you feel you've heard how much pitch variety your voice is capable of, try the same exercise with the opening passage of your own speech. For maximum pitch variation, try singing the passage, if you dare. Don't worry about making sense, just give yourself as much vocal freedom as you can. Repeat the passage several times. Gradually return to speaking the words in a meaningful way, but continue to use variations in pitch to color your ideas. Tape your speech again, and see if you can hear the difference.

Meaningful tempo variety can be achieved in very much the same way. Once again, read the JFK passage aloud. Your job is to complete the passage and drive your points home, first using a full forty-five seconds, then in thirty seconds, then in just twenty seconds. Once you've tried all three variations, take a moment to reflect on the way in which changes in pace affected the overall tone of your communication. Did accelerating the tempo increase the urgency of the message? Or did it obscure important points? Take a look at your own speech passage and find at least one place where it might be appropriate to pick up the tempo and one where it would help to slow it down. Read the passage again into the tape recorder and note where adding tempo variety strengthens your message.

Once you've experimented for a while with deliberately varying pitch and tempo to enhance your message, you'll probably find yourself doing it naturally as you continue to rehearse.

OVEREMPHATIC DELIVERY

While some speakers inadvertently project a lack of enthusiasm for their message, others find they have the opposite problem: Everything they say sounds *too* important. Larger meanings are lost because each word is receiving too much value in the delivery. As with any repeated cadence, it gets monotonous for the audience pretty fast.

If you suspect you may have this problem, experimenting with the pitch and tempo exercises above will help, but you'll probably want to work in reverse. Instead of emphasizing the underlined words, try to de-emphasize (through subtle changes in pitch, tempo, or volume) what's not underlined.

In some instances, overemphatic delivery occurs because the speaker is "punching" ideas into the listeners' brains through volume emphasis. ("In a FREE society, ART is not a WEAPON and it does NOT BELONG to the SPHERE of POLEMICS or IDEOLOGY.") If this is your tendency, imagine instead that you can gently "lift" important ideas into their minds by changing your pitch. This subtle adjustment gives the listener room to consider and internally respond to what you are saying rather than being barraged by a series of verbal blows.

LACK OF RESONANCE

If you think your voice seems shrill, nasal, or thin, you may need to adjust where your sound is coming from. The best way to counteract these tendencies is to open up your throat while you speak, the way singers do when they sing. We all instinctively know how to open up our throats: We do it every time we yawn or the doctor tells us to say "aaaah." You can teach yourself to open your throat during public speaking simply by practicing yawning while you talk.

Say the following sentence aloud: "Neil made mounds of money mining moonbeams."

Now simulate a yawn (or do a real one if you can). Repeat the sentence aloud, beginning it while you are still yawning.

Did the words sound deeper and more resonant even after you stopped yawning? If so, it's because the breath was unimpeded as it traveled over your vocal cords. Repeat this exercise three times.

Now say the sentence several times without yawning, but try to maintain that "open throat" feeling. You might find that you need to open your mouth a little wider than you are used to. This may feel strange at first, but soon you'll see that your sound is actually flowing more freely, giving your voice more power.

UMMING AND AHHHING

If you tend to ramble or find yourself constantly filling space with *ums* and *ahs,* you may be consciously or unconsciously afraid of silence. In general, the listener's mind needs more time to process speech than the speaker's mind needs to create it. So take your time. Let your points land. Instead of filling pauses with meaningless sound or rambling, simply breathe calmly and connect to your audience for a moment. This gives you time to think about what you want to say next and sends the message that you are totally in control rather than rushed or pressured. It will also help your audience understand where one thought ends and a new one begins. As long as your pauses are meaningfully filled—that is, you maintain an active connection with the audience through the silence—you won't be in danger of losing their attention. If you need more practice with the concept of the filled pause, go back and reexplore the Start–Stop Exercise (p. 64).

CONFIDENT COMMUNICATION

These exercises should help give you confidence in your ability to communicate well. If you're not yet satisfied with your progress, set aside time in the near future to try some of the exercises again. If you keep in mind that everything you do or say is an action in pursuit of your objective and that your listeners, therefore, must understand every idea fully, just a little practice is all that will be necessary.

As you listen to yourself on tape, continually ask yourself which parts sound the best to you—that is, which parts most strongly communicate the message. These are the parts to concentrate on.

Ask yourself how it feels to speak in the way you most like to hear yourself. At first it may feel awkward and unnatural, but with a little practice you can assimilate a few new vocal habits that will ultimately be just as natural and much more powerful than your unexamined, habitual way of speaking. Actors do it all the time.

THE SUCCESSFUL SPEAKING IMAGE

Now that you've taken the time to deconstruct your physical and vocal self-presentation, you need to put it all back together. What the audience receives from you over the course of a speech is not just your words, your body language, and your vocal delivery but an overall sense of who you are. From the moment you take the stage, everything you do and say contributes to the total image you project behind the podium.

While image may not be everything, it is an important tool in your pursuit of your objective, whatever that objective may be. To state the obvious, speakers who project a likable, sincere, expert image are far more likely to win the trust of their listeners than those who appear shy, elusive, or condescending. The image you project as a speaker is so significant, in fact, that it is often remembered long after the specific words you have presented are forgotten.

It's important here to differentiate between image and personality. In spite of their similarities, they are not interchangeable constructs—which should be good news for anyone who self-identifies as "shy" in real life but would like to be seen as outgoing and confident on stage. We see this phenomenon in the acting world all the time: For example, Robert De Niro, well-known for his introverted demeanor, has no problem projecting a powerful image on the big screen. That's because, while personality refers to the entire complex of a person's behavioral and emotional characteristics, image can be consciously *created* by the selection and presentation of particular traits or characteristics. When creating an extroverted role, De Niro actively calls forth parts of himself that may remain hidden in his daily interactions with friends, family, reporters, or the general public.

Instead of associating image with who you are and what you feel, it may be more useful to look at it in terms of what role you are playing at a particular moment. In other words, how do you want your audience to perceive you: as a motivator, a truth-teller, a teacher, an objective expert, an insider, a friend? The image you project will be inextricably tied to the role you have chosen. If you are playing the role of inspirational speaker, you might find yourself buoyantly striding to the podium, taking in your audience with a bright smile from your first moment of contact, projecting an image of someone who can't wait to share something he is really excited about. These behaviors, however, will probably be inappropriate if you are playing the role of a truth-teller who must force people to accept the hard realities of budget cutbacks and personnel layoffs. Here you might approach the podium with a dignified sense of purpose, your eye contact suggesting that you understand and empathize with the pain your message will cause your audience, projecting an image of someone who cares enough about them to say the difficult things.

Giving some thought to the role you are playing and the image you project doesn't make you a phony; it simply allows you to control the variables of self-presentation, ensuring that the impression you make is consistent with the message you are sending. Only when you fail to commit to the role you are playing—in other words, if you become a bad actor and don't really believe what you're communicating—do you risk creating an inauthentic relationship with your audience.

Cultivating Your Image

There's a big difference between self-image and the image the audience sees. Everyone tends to be more aware of their own faults and idiosyncrasies than others will be. It's easy to get discouraged if you think you're too short to command respect, you're too young to project authority, or your voice is too gravelly to draw your listeners in. But where would Napoleon, Joan of Arc, and Louis Armstrong be if they'd let these petty worries stop them?

There is no prototype for the "perfect speaker." Different speakers appeal to different audiences for different reasons. You shouldn't, therefore, try to be all things to all people. Just look at the career of someone like Rosie O'Donnell. By her own admission, she is a performer of limited range. In role after role—from *Sleepless in Seattle* and *A League of Their Own* to her stint in *Grease* on Broadway—she basically plays herself, and she does it really well. In fact, she not only parlayed her witty tough-girl-next-door banter into a hit movie career but also turned herself into one of the most popular talk show hosts on television. Rosie knows a secret that we would all do well to learn: Audiences appreciate people who are comfortable being themselves in public and who know how to make an asset out of who they really are.

But what if you're not so comfortable with the public persona you project? Take heart, because the successful speaking image is something that can be cultivated. Just as with everything we do, we project certain things about ourselves by habit. If you want to learn how to project new qualities, you'll need to practice new habits.

One way to do that is by modeling behaviors you like. Experienced actors understand that observation and imitation are powerful tools for projecting personality. Olivier himself confessed that he "unashamedly" copied the qualities of colleagues he admired. So take some time to identify the qualities and habits of speakers you like—coworkers, TV and radio personalities, politicians, whoever—then try incorporating those traits into your own speech delivery. It might feel strange at first, but the more you work with these habits, the more natural they'll start to feel. Try not to reject anything out of hand. How will you know it's "not you" until you've tried it on?

Sartorial Splendor

In the professional theater, actors and costume designers often work together to come up with the "look" that's right for the character. In the speaking arena, you are, of course, both the performer and the designer (which should dramatically cut down on the number of diva fits you'll be throwing in the dressing room).

Finding the look that's right for the role you're playing is an important part of projecting the successful speaking image, and requires a little forethought. While clothes may not make the man or woman, they certainly tell a lot about the person who wears them—so what do you want to tell your audience?

For most speaking engagements in the business world, you'll want to tell them that you are a competent professional who understands the importance of the speaking occasion. That means wearing business clothes (suits, probably) that fit well, are clean and neatly pressed, and reflect the professional styles of the day. While your clothing should be attractive, it shouldn't upstage you. If your audience remembers your costume more than your message, you've picked the wrong outfit. Most important, to project confidence, you need to like the way you look in your clothes and be comfortable moving around in them. Wearing expensive new shoes with six-inch heels that you can't walk in won't enhance your message, no matter how *haute couture* the designer label may be. And overstarched Oxford shirts that cut off the blood supply to your brain will likely prove a distraction, for you and for the audience!

So use common sense. A general rule of thumb is that you should look like your audience, only slightly better. If you're in doubt about what might be appropriate, err on the side of conservatism—no one will fault you for wearing a suit and tie when khakis and a blazer would have sufficed, but you can be sure that this principle does not work in reverse.

A few words about makeup. Men: Don't wear any. Women: In general, your "street" makeup (what you wear every day) should suffice. If you're speaking in a very large hall, consider using slightly more than you normally would around your eyes, but beware of overdoing it (you'll probably be talking to people one on one after you finish your presentation and you don't want to look clownish). If you don't usually wear makeup, consider applying the following cosmetics in subtle earth tones, simply to accentuate your features under the lights: eye shadow, eyeliner, mascara, blush, and lipstick. This should give you a natural, healthy appearance without making you appear made up. Finally, if you're speaking under bright lights or have a tendency to perspire when you perform, apply a little powder over your finished makeup.

Experiment with your costume and makeup in advance. Once you see how successfully you can look the part of the confident professional speaker, you'll probably feel more like one, too.

Chapter 7

Stage Fright

"Acting is standing up naked and turning around very slowly."

—ROSALIND RUSSELL

ACTOR WILLIAM HURT WAS ONCE SO NERVOUS HIS LIPS literally locked during a performance. In his own words: "I had to turn away from the audience to pry my mouth open with my fingers."

While Hurt's was clearly an extreme case, almost everyone who does business in the public eye struggles with nerves at one time or another. Barbra Streisand's fear of public performing is legendary. Michael Jordan admits to regularly experiencing pre-game jitters. Even Ronald Reagan, "The Great Communicator," confessed to getting "puckered up" before every big speech.

And the list goes on and on. You may be surprised to learn that many of the greatest speakers and performers of all time have been admitted stage-fright sufferers, including George Burns, Johnny Carson, Harrison Ford, Dustin Hoffman, Liza Minelli, Paul Newman, Sidney Poitier, Carly Simon, Gloria Steinem, Harry Truman, and Oprah Winfrey. Even Cicero, perhaps the greatest orator ever, was known to shake visibly when he stood up in front of a crowd.

While the physical manifestations of stage fright can be alarming at first, seasoned professionals know that butterflies simply come with the territory. It's the body's way of acknowledging that you're about to do something important, something exciting. On the plus side, you get a little extra boost of adrenaline to put you at the top of your game; on the minus, the excess adrenaline can result in a heightened experience of anxiety if it's not put to good use. Knowing how to channel and use those butterflies effectively is what this chapter's all about.

FEAR ITSELF

A notorious survey informed the world that Americans, on average, fear public speaking more than death—prompting comedian Jerry Seinfeld to observe that most people would rather be in the casket than delivering the eulogy. Although in practice this may be an exaggeration (given the choice of dropping dead or delivering a speech, most people would probably choose the latter), it's undeniably true that giving a speech can be a very frightening experience.

What sets accomplished performers apart isn't so much that they don't experience jitters but rather that they aren't debilitated by them. According to *All in the Family* star Carroll O'Connor, "A professional actor has a kind of tension. The amateur is thrown by it, but the professional needs it." He's talking about the upside of fear: Being a little nervous gives you the edge you need to pull off a high-stakes performance.

When you get right down to it, there's not much physiological difference between fear and excitement. Both are "fight-or-flight" responses, readying us to take action. Both fear and excitement result in heightened blood sugar, dilated pupils, increased need for oxygen, accelerated heart rate, and that going-down-in-the-elevator feeling in your stomach. The real difference is psychological: When we think of it as fear, it makes us feel sick, whereas when we think of it as excitement, we feel elated. There's really no reason, of course, to fight *or* take flight in the speaking situation—the audience only *seems* like a predator. So you have a choice. You can decide that old familiar feeling is paralyzing fear or you can do as the actors do and call it "performance energy." It's up to you.

THE POWER OF PREPARATION

Without a doubt, the greatest antidote to performance anxiety is solid preparation. Basketball great Michael Jordan handles nerves by falling back on basic moves he's mastered through hours of hard work. "If you practice, practice, practice," His Airness says, "you let those things take over when you get nervous."

And that's the reason why actors don't get all hung up about stage fright, either: They know they've been through an intensive rehearsal process that will serve them well when they're in the moment of performance. They know the text inside and out—they're clear about their actions and objectives, as well as their physical blocking, verbal delivery, and use of props—so there's very little left to chance when they get in front of an audience. This frees them up to be in the moment, connecting to the other characters and to the audience, rather than being overly concerned with how they just executed their last line or what difficult piece of stage business is coming up next.

Through the first six chapters of this book you created a similar rehearsal process for yourself, focusing on what you are going to say, why your audience needs to hear it, and how your verbal and physical behavior can best communicate your message. So if you've been working on the ideas and trying out the exercises, you're well on your way to putting nerves in their place.

Now, if you've been putting off rehearsing (because the event is still pretty far away, you can't find the right place, you're just too darned busy, or some other lame excuse you've been giving yourself), you may be a victim of stage fright and not even know it. Many people use avoidance to deal with performance anxiety. Since preparing for the event evokes fear, they just skip the preparation. Skipping the preparation, of course, only intensifies the fear. It's a vicious, nausea-inducing circle.

Think of rehearsal like going to the gym. You may dread the thought when you're rolling out of bed at six in the morning, but after you've finished your workout, you feel great.

YOUR INNER MONOLOGUE

But why is public speaking so frightening, anyway? Are we really afraid of "falling flat on our faces" as the saying goes? (The odds of slipping at the podium and falling splat onto the stage are, after all, fairly slim.) Or are we afraid of rejection by our colleagues, being exposed as a fraud, confronting the unknown?

Considering how much power we let these fears have over us, it's amazing how vague and general they tend to be. It's usually difficult for people to put into words what makes them nervous about public speaking. What exactly is the worst that could happen—the thing that makes your stomach tighten and your skin get clammy at the mere thought of giving a speech?

Destroying the Destructive Inner Monologue

Most of the fears people have about public speaking situations are irrational. But if you know your enemies, it's easier to conquer them. Here's an exercise intended to identify and debunk the irrational fears that are getting in your way.

Write a first-person monologue in which you describe your worst conceivable public speaking scenario. How bad could it get, in the worst of all possible worlds? This is your chance to get your absolute worst nightmare out of your subconscious and down on paper.

Be specific. If you need help, use the following sentence fragments to spark your imagination. Then let your fears run wild and write for five minutes without stopping.

I wake up on the morning of the speech and . . .

As I'm about to leave my house I realize . . .

When I get to the space . . .

As the speaker before me is introduced, I discover . . .

When I walk to the podium I . . .

My mind is . . .

I start speaking and . . .

I notice that the audience is . . .

I react by . . .

As I continue to talk I realize . . .

I finish speaking and . . .

At the end of the day I pick up my evaluations, one of which
   says . . .

Good. There it all is in black and white.

Method Versus Madness

Now let's examine what you've written.

Go back and cross out anything you wrote that is highly unlikely to happen. These may have arisen because of fears you have in other situations, but if you're honest with yourself, you'll realize they're nothing to worry about in an actual public speaking setting. It's time to admit that these fears are *irrational*. Scratch them out completely.

For example, if you wrote, "In the most serious part of my speech, someone in the audience laughs out loud," ask yourself if you've ever been in an audience so rude that they laughed inappropriately at the speaker. It's extremely rare. Do you think you're so special that your speech will be the one-in-a-million exception? It's *irrational*. Scratch it out.

Once you've crossed out everything that is pretty much out of the realm of actual possibility—the irrational fears—you may well be left with some rational ones. These are the things you're afraid might really happen when you give a speech.

Rational fears demand rational solutions, and luckily one can always be found.

For example, if you're afraid that the podium will be too high, get to the space early and find out how to adjust it or, at the very least, where you can get a booster step. If you're afraid your hands will shake, plan to rest them on the podium or steady your notes by holding them close to your body. Worried you'll have a coughing fit just as you get to the speech climax? Have a glass of water next to you and allow yourself to pause for a drink while the fit passes. No big deal. Your audience knows you're a human being, after all.

Some fears can be eliminated right away. Coffee-stained notes can be avoided by making sure you have lots of copies handy and by not bringing all of them to the breakfast table. If you're worried you'll oversleep and be late for the speaking engagement, go out and buy an extra alarm clock or arrange for a friend to call you early in the morning.

Fears that your audience will be against you or will perceive you as an impostor are very common, but rarely founded. Try seeing it from your audience's point of view and you'll realize how much they're actually on your side. Think of a time when you've been an audience member at a lecture. What did you want from the speaker? To learn something? To be transported? To be stimulated? Probably *not* to test the speaker's knowledge or see him make a fool of himself.

Your audience isn't there to judge you but to gain insight. And providing insight doesn't mean knowing everything about everything. You just need to have a little special knowledge to impart on the particular topic you are addressing. In the words of Will Rogers, "Everybody is ignorant, only on different subjects." Remember, you're prepared to speak on this subject; your audience is not. They are more than willing to give you the benefit of the doubt as long as you give them a meaningful experience they can use.

So look again at each fear sentence you haven't crossed out, and decide on a realistic way to handle the situation. Write your solutions down, so you'll remember them.

Fostering the Constructive Inner Monologue

Of course, even the things you labeled "rational" fears are not likely to happen, in most cases. In fact, the speech will probably go very much the way you've rehearsed it and may well earn rave reviews.

So let's start thinking positively. How good could this experience possibly be?

What if this speech turned out to be a highlight of your personal or professional life? What would the speaking experience be like?

Take a few minutes to visualize yourself wowing an audience with your speech. How did you look when you walked onto the stage or into the conference room? What was your first indication that it was going well? What was going on in your mind before, during, and after the speech? What was the best part? How did you know they were with you? What did they do when you finished? What feedback did you get? Create a vivid mental picture of your performance and the enthusiastic audience response.

Once you've intoxicated yourself with the sweet smell of success, do the following exercise: Write a short letter to a close friend or colleague about your imagined public speaking triumph, describing in detail what a big hit you were. (Make sure the recipient of this imaginary letter is someone you wouldn't be afraid to brag to. Modesty is definitely not the objective here.) Write for five minutes, as freely and as quickly as you can, without stopping to think or judge what you've written.

Go.

As you wrote your letter, did you conjure up a mental picture of how you performed? Did you feel what it was like to enjoy the speaking experience? Were you able to see the impact of your message on the audience?

These are important sensations to remember as you continue preparing for your speech. It's easy to let your thoughts wander off to all the things that might go wrong. Counteract this tendency by spending a little time each day focusing on all the things that might go right. When you imagine success, you vastly increase the likelihood that the real thing will soon follow.

READINESS AND RELAXATION

Okay, you've done the visualizing success thing and, well, quite honestly, there are still some lingering jitters. Remember, it's okay to experience nerves, you just need to know how to rechannel that nervous energy into constructive energy. Since some of the most debilitating manifestations of stage fright are physiological—shallow breathing, shakes, queasiness—one of the best ways to alleviate the symptoms is to practice restoring physical calm.

The acting profession has developed a reliable ritual for constructively rechanneling the physical symptoms of nervousness: the warm-up routine. Done before most big rehearsals and every performance, the warm-up gets the blood flowing, regulates the heart and breathing rates so that energy is used as efficiently as possible, and tunes the "instruments" of communication.

The warm-up should become a regular part of your speech rehearsal routine. Before each run-through, perform this entire series of exercises. That way your body will get used to starting the speech in a state of relaxation and readiness. On the day of your actual performance, do this routine before you leave the house, to center yourself and get your energy flowing in the right direction. You can even slip discreetly into the restroom at the designated speaking place and do somewhat more contained versions of the exercises right before you take the stage. Your performance will benefit enormously and no one will be the wiser.

Warm-Up 1: Deep Breathing

Lie on your back with your eyes closed and place a hand on your stomach. Take a deep breath and let it out. You should notice your hand rising on the inhale and falling on the exhale. Keep taking deep breaths until you've relaxed into this pattern of expanding on the inhale and contracting on the exhale.

Don't rush through this experience. This is time you've set aside for yourself simply to enjoy the feeling of breathing deeply. It should feel comfortable and relaxing.

Stay on the floor, just breathing, for at least three minutes. Then slowly come to an upright sitting position. Stay in this position for at least one minute before getting to your feet.

Warm-Up 2: Full-Body Tense and Relax

Stand in a relaxed, upright position. Tense your arms, take a deep breath in, and hold the tension for a count of five. Then relax your arms and exhale. Repeat the tense–relax cycle with your shoulders, hands, lower back, buttocks, legs, and feet, breathing deeply all the while.

It also helps to tense and relax your face. Open your eyes and mouth as wide as you can. Then relax. Now squeeze the muscles in your face as tight as you can, then relax. Repeat this exercise three times.

Finally, shake out your whole body. Imagine that you are throwing out the tension that was trapped inside. Breathe deeply and relax.

Warm-Up 3: The Rag Doll

The Rag Doll Exercise will clear your mind, relax your body, and help you find a comfortable, straight-up posture.

Stand with your feet shoulder width apart. Imagine that your head has become very heavy and let your chin drop to your chest. Now, let the weight of your head slowly pull you toward the ground, one vertebra at a time, until you are bent all the way over, like a rag doll. Be sure to release your neck so that it feels loose and wobbly. While you are bent over, gently sway back and forth. Don't forget to breathe.

When you have fully relaxed into this position, gently begin to roll up—from the back of your knees, through your buttocks, and all the way through your spine—one vertebra at a time. The last thing to come up should be your head.

Once you are upright, take a deep breath and relax your shoulders on the exhale. Repeat this exercise three times.

Warm-Up 4: Aerobic Exercise

A great way to relieve stress that gets trapped in your body is through vigorous physical exercise. In addition to the relaxation and posture warm-ups already described, incorporate some kind of cardiovascular exercise into your rehearsal routine. Try doing fifty jumping jacks (counting each one out loud) or a three-minute high-impact aerobic routine right before you run through your speech. You'll soon discover that after your body has been put through a workout, it doesn't have the energy to be tense. Your breathing will automatically become deeper and your muscles more relaxed.

Don't forget: Public speaking is a physical activity. Physical training will give you the body awareness and availability you'll need to perform at your peak.

ATTITUDE ADJUSTMENT

When asked if she got nervous singing on Broadway, Ethel Merman supposedly replied, "Me get nervous? They paid twenty-five dollars a seat; let *them* get nervous!" (At today's prices, they should be terrified.) But all kidding aside, she makes a great point: It's your show and you're the one in control. Remember, they've come to learn from you, not to pass judgment. Simply keeping that in mind at the top of your speech should help quell the butterflies.

If you just can't shake the image of the audience as an angry mob destined to see you fail, try thinking about your relationship with them in a new way. Remember what a powerful tool the imagination is. As you look out over the crowd, imagine that they are a class of bright students eager to learn about a favorite subject you are teaching, or job candidates hoping you'll pluck them out of the crowd and put them to work for your company. Use the creative visualization to remind yourself that you're the one with the power.

Here's another theatrical principle to keep in mind if you're overly concerned with what your listeners might think of you: The audience sees only what's there, not what's not.

Because actors spend a lot of time rehearsing a play, making lots of character choices that they will ultimately discard in the later stages of the process, they can get very hung up on all the things they're not doing. On opening night, it's common to hear actors in the dressing room obsessing about all the choices they've thrown away and how the story of the play will no longer make sense to the audience. And yet, magically, the audience always seems to feel the story they saw was the complete one. With the possible exception of a theater critic seeing *Hamlet* for the seventy-fourth time, the people in the audience won't even know what they're not getting—unless the actors tell them.

The same holds true for public speaking. Your audience will see only what's there; they won't miss what's not there unless you, in word or tone, apologize for what you aren't giving them. Because of your good preparation, there's a lot you know and a lot you can do. Focus on that. In the moments before you go on, ignore what you feel you don't know and can't do. Your audience will never even know about it.

If you still can't keep your mind from perseverating on negative thoughts before you get up to speak, here's another remedy: Picture a friend or a coach congratulating you on the great performance you are about to give. Or take a moment and imagine a loved one holding your hand or rubbing your back. Get your mind off the million things you're worried about that aren't really going to happen and start thinking about something constructive.

An old actor's trick for the few moments right before the curtain rises is to think about a favorite line or moment from the play: the thing you can't wait to get out there and do. Do the same with your speech. Concentrate on the best part and how much they're going to appreciate hearing it.

Finally, if you're worried that the audience is going to see how nervous you are, never fear. As talk show host Dick Cavett once remarked, everything you do in performance "looks better than it feels." Although it can be hard to believe, most symptoms of stage fright are completely undetectable by the audience.

So relax.

Chapter 8

Late Rehearsals

"The more you work, the more you find."
—Robert Sean Leonard

As you incorporate imagination exercises, intensive text analysis, and new physical and vocal habits into your presentation, your performance will deepen and strengthen, grow in clarity and persuasiveness, and continue to progress toward the best it can be. That means it will be getting closer and closer to some final "shape." The analogy to live theater is that once the actors reach opening night, they know what to say, where to move, and how they will work to affect the other characters in the play. By the time there's a real audience, they've stretched themselves in lots of ways and made some choices about which results they want to keep. They have a lot to hold on to.

That is not to say, however, that the performance becomes static. Concentrating on keeping it exactly the same night after night is the best way to drain the life out of any show. It's also futile, because the presence of live human beings guarantees that there will always be a certain amount of variation from rehearsal to rehearsal and performance to performance, at least in subtle ways. And that's a good thing, because that subtlety is what gives any live performance its "aliveness."

When speakers worry about being overrehearsed, what they're really afraid of is losing that subtlety and aliveness, and replacing it with rigidity. That doesn't happen to actors who know how to rehearse, and it doesn't have to happen to you. The last stages of the rehearsal process are all about reconnecting to what's exciting about your speech and building the momentum that will carry you into performance. They are also about preparing yourself to be on the set, getting your written and visual materials in order, and making clear decisions about when and how you'll use them.

POLISHING YOUR ROUTINE

Up until now, you've been encouraged to break your speech down into its component parts and examine it from every angle. As your performance date nears, however, it's time to start putting it all back together. Between now and when you actually give the speech, find as many large chunks of rehearsal time as you can, so you can run longer sections of the speech and sometimes do it in its entirety.

It's best to develop a dependable routine. It would be ideal to rehearse every day at the same time. That's hard to fit into most people's schedules, but the point is to establish as much regularity as possible. Always begin with your warm-up, and commit to making the most of your rehearsal time. Lock the doors and unplug the phones, if necessary.

A clear routine helps in several ways. It develops the habit of speaking at an appointed time, which will ultimately make it easier to deliver the goods at curtain time whether you're in the mood or not. Sticking to a schedule also helps you get more rehearsing in, because if you get in the habit of waiting until you have free time, you'll discover you never have any. Finally, knowing when, where, and how you're going to rehearse takes away many of the unknowns that lead to nervousness and can help you develop the habit of being comfortable rather than hassled behind the podium. In short, regularity promotes professionalism.

Space and Time

From here on out, every time you rehearse you must have a clear sense of the space you'll actually be speaking in. That means if your presentation will ultimately take place in an auditorium, but you'll be rehearsing in your living room, you need to activate your imagination so you'll be prepared for the real thing.

If you don't yet know what kind of space you'll be speaking in, it's time to find out. Call whoever is in charge of the event and ask about the size and setup of the room. How far will you be from the audience? Will you be on a stage? What are the acoustics like? Will you have a microphone? A podium?

If you don't have accurate answers to these questions yet, you may be making some assumptions that you'll be sorry you made. Calling the people in charge will not only get your questions answered but will also make them feel that you really care about what you're doing for them.

Even better than a phone call would be a visit. If you can check out the actual room well before the date of your presentation—study the layout and get a feel for the place—there will be a lot less to worry about when the date comes.

Once you have a basic idea of what the space is like, actively incorporate that knowledge into your rehearsals by simulating the actual speaking scenario as closely as possible. If you're going to have a podium, rehearse with a podium. If you don't have one and you're mechanically inclined, you can pretty easily rig one out of some cardboard and masking tape. (If you're not mechanically inclined, maybe you can get someone to do it for you.) Or use a stack of books on a table. Just do your best to re-create what you think it will be like.

If you will be using a microphone, it doesn't hurt to practice with one if you can. Just remember, though, not to let the microphone do your work for you. It's better to turn down the volume and project into the mike than to electronically amplify a low-energy voice.

Whether or not you'll be using a microphone, if the space you'll be speaking in is larger than the one you rehearse in, use your imagination to knock out some walls. As the date of your performance draws near, it becomes more important than ever to ingrain the appropriate habits by projecting your voice and making eye contact throughout an imaginary auditorium.

You should also know by now the exact amount of time you'll be expected to speak. If there's any question about it, check with the organizers. Time yourself in rehearsal and make sure you come in *under* the time allotted. Unless you're an unusually slow speaker, you probably don't want to speed up your delivery, but you shouldn't hesitate to cut out whole chunks of your speech (even chunks you love, if necessary) if there's any chance you'll run long. You don't want to overstay your welcome, no matter how important your message or how eloquent your words. As they say in show biz: Always leave 'em wanting more.

Preparing Your Script and Notes

At this point you know whether you'll be using a fully written-out speech, note cards, or something in between. It helps to have these materials prepared the way you want them well in advance of your presentation date.

If you're working from a script, use sturdy (sixty-pound) white paper and a large font (at least twelve-point), so the pages are easy to handle and the print is easy to read. Double space and leave wide margins. Make sure the paragraph breaks are easy to see—they may signify a change in your action. Feel free to mark the script up, to remind yourself of key words or other important information about what you should be focusing on in different parts of the speech. And don't forget to number the pages, in case you drop them.

When you're typing up your script, avoid ending a page in the middle of a thought. If a sentence begins on the bottom of a page but doesn't end there, shift the whole thing to the next page. Also, when you're in performance, rather than turning pages over when you're done with them, try simply sliding them off to the left. Many speakers feel this is a less obtrusive movement and less distracting to the audience.

If you're using notes, follow the same advice about sturdy paper and large fonts (or handwriting). You may find you depend on your notes less and less as you rehearse. If so, try reducing the number of notes you bring with you. Fewer notes will make it easier to keep your attention on the audience, where it belongs. Of course, if you're more comfortable with a lot of notes, use a lot of notes.

By the way, if you're using a script or notes, please don't pretend you aren't. Many speakers act as though their scripts or note cards are a dirty little secret to be kept hidden at all costs. If you're using a script or notes, the audience will know that. They're not blind or stupid. And they also don't care. If they were up there, they'd probably be using them, too. If you use the written materials as a way of helping you connect effectively with your audience, there's no need to feel the least bit guilty about them. Use them with pride.

That said, there are two places where you want to make extra sure that you will not be overly dependent on notes or a script. The very beginning and the very end are such crucial elements of your presentation that they should usually be committed to memory. Of course, if your speech is very short, you may want to memorize the whole thing.

Try to Remember

"How do you remember all those lines?" It's the question most often asked of stage actors, and it always strikes us as kind of funny. After all, it's just about the least interesting thing we do in our craft. And once you've done it a lot, it's also one of the easiest. Yet, to nonperformers, the ability to memorize can seem as mysterious as if we had X-ray vision.

So, at the risk of giving away all of our secrets, here are a few tried-and-true actor's tricks for remembering your lines:

- Commit the first sentence or phrase to memory, repeat it in your head, then check to see if you were right. If you were, move on to the next sentence, but don't go any further until you can do the first two in sequence, flawlessly. Continue in this fashion, always starting back at the beginning, so you memorize not only the sentences, but also the way in which they fit together.

- Write it out longhand. This makes you take the time to concentrate on each word, see them all in a new form, and reinforce your memory of them through a physical activity.

- Tape record the portion you want to memorize and listen to it in the car or the tub.

- Associate the words with vivid, easily recalled images. For example, if you're having trouble remembering "Italy rejected Churchill's offer," you might develop a strong mental picture of an Italy-shaped boot kicking a caricature of Churchill into the Atlantic.

- Work on memorizing the script right before you go to sleep at night. You'll be amazed at how much you retain in the morning. Also, many short memorization sessions are better than a few long ones, so plan to do a little bit every night.

- Rehearse, rehearse, rehearse. The more you say something out loud, the easier it will be to remember.

WORKING WITH VISUALS

As we discussed in chapter 3, visual aids can add clarity, power, and entertainment value to many kinds of speeches. They also, unfortunately, have the potential to distract from your message if handled inexpertly.

Not surprisingly, visual aids do not speak for themselves. You're the only speaker in the room, and you have a responsibility to help your aids actually aid you, not just in the planning stages but during the presentation as well. How you use the slides is just as important as what's on them.

Once you get to the point where you're running large portions of the speech, you should incorporate your visuals into every rehearsal. They're not a separate, simultaneous show, but an integral part of the presentation, so don't expect them to take care of themselves at the last minute.

Double Exposure

Part of the potential problem with visuals is that the slides may steal the show. No actor worth his salt will allow himself to be upstaged by a prop, and neither should you.

This isn't just about slides that are especially eye-catching, either. *Every* slide competes for the audience's attention. At any moment, each person in the audience has to decide whether to look at you or at the slide. Although this may sound like a trivial concern, this split focus can garble your message. You need to help them make the choice that will keep their attention where you want it.

Giving and taking focus is a big issue for stage actors. It's not much of an issue at all for television and movie actors, because in screen work the camera tells the audience where to look. But on the stage, if a lot is going on stage left, the audience will be paying less attention to what's going on stage right, even if the stage right stuff is more important to the play. Actors need to learn how to draw the audience's attention to them and how to direct it onto others when necessary to serve the purposes of the play. It takes practice, and a high level of awareness of everything that's going on.

You need to similarly orchestrate the audience's attention to help them get the most out of your speech. Always remember: You know the speech and the slides much better than they do. They're hearing and seeing all this for the first time, and they will not understand it all instantaneously.

First Impressions Count

Before you can incorporate your slides into your presentation, you need to study each one to determine exactly what visual story it tells. Step back and try to imagine seeing this slide for the first time, as though you had no idea of its content and can see only its shapes and colors. If you were to say nothing at all, what do you think an audience would get from looking at this slide for a second or two? What purely visual information does it convey?

Do you see concentric circles? If so, that suggests that this slide is about a sequence of things contained inside each other. (Perhaps an individual at the center, inside a workgroup, inside a department, inside a subsidiary, inside a company.) A very specific kind of relationship between elements is presented visually.

Is the main thing that jumps out at you a line rising from left to right? We all know enough about graphs to realize that this visual information is probably about some kind of increase.

Do you immediately notice a red area and a green area? Two things are being compared and/or contrasted.

Other visual first impressions might include one bar of a bar graph towering over the others, arrows indicating a succession of steps in some process, or a striking similarity among the objects presented on the screen. Or you might notice one part of the text in bold or larger type than the rest, or the sheer length of a list.

As we've discussed, public speakers can get so caught up in what they themselves are doing that they forget that everything they do must be for the benefit of their listeners. Failure to put yourself in the audience's shoes when it comes to visuals is a grave example of that kind of mistake. Remember: You know what the slide is supposed to be about, so you're going to have a tendency to assume the audience does, too. But they don't.

Go through and describe what you might reasonably expect to be the audience's first impression of every slide. Then ask yourself for each one how well the visual information reinforces your message. Does the visual first impression of what's important on a slide correspond to the point you're trying to make with that slide? If so, great: You're working in concert with your visual aids. If the correspondence is not strong—for example, if the important thing about a graph seems to be that it's rising from left to right, but what's really significant is how low it started out—it's not necessarily an insurmountable difficulty, but you need to be aware that when that slide comes up on the screen, you're going to have to work extra hard to orient the audience to see it the way you want them to. To accomplish this, you might decide to add a couple of lines like, "As you can see, we've experienced substantial growth this year. But what's most remarkable is the baseline from which we started, which is represented in the lower-left-hand corner."

Then take the next step and go beyond first impressions. If they were to get everything they could possibly get out of this particular slide, what would that be? There's a vital question that often goes unasked: *Exactly why is this slide part of this presentation?* If you can answer that question, in detail, and in terms of what the audience can and should get out of it—then, and only then, you'll be able to use the slide effectively to benefit your presentation.

Graphs

Whenever you bring a graph up on the screen, the next thing you should do is to tell us what the x- and y-axes represent. Far too many speakers assume the audience will see how the axes are labeled, and they decide that telling them that information is talking down to them. Not so. A graph is a complicated object. When the audience sees one for the first time they're taking in a lot of visual stimuli and listening to you talk at the same time. They try desperately to put the whole thing together to figure out what they're supposed to get out of it. No one will feel talked down to if you help acclimate them to what they're seeing. And if you *don't* tell them, they may well get confused and lose track of your argument as they try to acclimate themselves.

Make sure you know exactly how you would want the audience to answer the question, "What was the point of that graph?" Having a vague sense of what the point is will not do.

Let's say you have a complex line graph that demonstrates, on a month-by-month basis, the total number of homicides, the total number of petty crimes, and the total amount of criminal activity in your police precinct over the past three years. The reason you've included it is that you want the city council to recognize that even though the total amount of criminal activity in your area has decreased, the number of homicides has actually increased, leading you to want more police protection. Instead of doing what most inexperienced speakers do and saying as soon as the slide pops up on the screen, "As you can see, the total amount of dangerous crime is actually up," take a few simple steps to orient your audience.

First, you need to tell them what they're looking at. "This graphic depicts trends in criminal activity in our precinct over the last thirty-six months." Good. Now they have a basic sense of what they'll be evaluating. Then you need to make sure they know how the statistics are being measured. "Time is on the horizontal axis; number of reported crimes, on the vertical." Next, acclimate them to the basic visual elements: "The red line represents the number of petty crimes reported; the blue line, the number of homicides; the green line, the total amount of criminal activity." Now they know which elements are being juxtaposed. At this point it makes perfect sense to let them know what the slide demonstrates. "As you can see, even though the total amount of criminal activity has decreased, only petty crime has actually gone down. The number of homicides per month has risen steadily for more than two years."

But your job doesn't end with a clear explanation of the image. Great speakers always tell their audiences what they should *do* with the graphic information they've received. "This graph clearly demonstrates that, contrary to what the police department is telling us, our residents are more likely to die on our streets today than they were three years ago. A more visible police presence on our streets, therefore, isn't a frivolous expenditure; it's a life-saving necessity."

Visual First Aid

Knowing why and how you are using each visual image to support the larger message of your speech is, of course, the most critical factor in determining the success of your visual presentation. But there are also technical factors that come into play. As you guide your audience through your visuals, the following tips will help you get the biggest bang for your visual aid buck:

- Never bring up a slide until you're ready for the audience's attention to go there. Many speakers click to the next slide when they're *finished* with the last one, instead of when they're really *ready* for the next one.

- Be sure to give the audience a very brief moment to take in the visual information of a slide before you start talking about it.

- If a slide has text on it, read some of it to help connect the slide to what you're saying. Speakers are often cautioned against reading the text on their slides, because it may seem to suggest that the audience does not know how to read it for themselves. But, again, you don't want to compete for the audience's attention while they're reading, and you don't want to lose their attention altogether by allowing for too long a moment of reading silence. The best way to deal with text slides, therefore, is to read aloud the major points, adding value to each one with a brief explanation or example.

- Address everything on the slide. If you completely ignore any portion of a slide, the audience's attention will zoom in on that portion and they'll wonder if you've made a mistake or—worse—may be hiding something from them. Why is it on the slide if you're not even going to refer to it? It's fine to address relatively unimportant portions of the slide with something like, "As you can see, we serve several other communities as well." In other words, if you don't want to go into detail about something, let the audience know that's a conscious decision, and give them at least a hint as to why you're not dealing with it fully.

- Point to parts of the slide to help the audience follow you. Or say, "As you can see in the upper right-hand corner . . ."

- If at all possible, stand close to the screen, so the audience redirects their gaze only minimally when looking back and forth between you and the slides. And, while you should refer to the screen to focus the audience's attention, don't talk directly to it. Remember, your conversation is with the audience, not with the props or the set.

BUILDING MOMENTUM

The Wile E. Coyote Theory of Public Speaking

Acting is an exercise in sustained concentration. There are no time-outs when you can ask the audience to ignore you for a minute while you pull yourself together. You have to be "on" the whole time, giving your all and maintaining focus.

The same goes for public speaking. You're allowed to cough or trip over a line now and then—no one will hold it against you—but if you allow anything to throw you, the speech will suffer. Maintaining your concentration gets harder and harder as a speech goes on, because you get tired. That's why it's important to rehearse the speech as a whole. It develops your ability to concentrate.

Now, you may feel you already know how to concentrate. You're not in second grade. But the kind of concentration required of actors and public speakers is of a higher order than you're probably used to.

If you haven't experienced anything like the following scenario yet, you almost certainly will at some point: You're behind the podium, the speech is going great, you're raising your left hand to scratch your cheek, and . . . WHAM! All you can think about is your left hand rising to scratch your cheek. Why is it doing that? Is it appropriate? Now the whole audience is watching me scratch my cheek. I can't believe I just scratched my cheek in front of all these people.

It sounds ridiculous until it's you up there. Maybe scratching your cheek wouldn't bother you. But maybe you get up there and instead of saying "Mr. Spalding met with Chad" you say "Mr. Spalding et with Jed." Now you're worried.

It's not that there's anything wrong with scratching your cheek or making accidental Beverly Hillbillies references. These things happen. The problem is in the worrying.

The creators of Looney Tunes had this psychological principle down pat. In almost every episode of the old *Roadrunner* cartoon, Wile E. Coyote finds himself chasing the Roadrunner off a cliff. But there doesn't seem to be any problem with that. He's running in midair. In fact, he would actually catch that darn Roadrunner except for one fatal mistake.

He looks down.

Once he looks down—stops to analyze what he's doing *while* he's doing it—he's doomed. He crashes to the ground in a cloud of dust.

In public speaking, looking down means allowing yourself to get distracted—by a hand rising to scratch your cheek, a fumbled phrase, a fear that your message is not being well received. In acting terms, you need to stay "in the moment," rather than allowing your-self to critique moments that have already passed or worry about moments that are still to come.

Don't look down. Keep forging on. Practice large sections of your speech at a time and don't allow yourself to stop and fix things. Imagine your audience so vividly that you won't do anything in front of them that you wouldn't do in front of a real audience. Keep going. No stopping to regroup, even minutely. With practice, you'll develop the kind of intense concentration, stamina, and momentum it takes to make it all the way across the gorge.

The Loop Exercise

Actors have an exercise designed to help them build the kind of momentum necessary to keep audiences with them every step of the way. It's called the Loop, and here's how it can work for you:

Pick a section of your speech to work on. The first time you do the exercise it should be at least a minute or two long, and up to, say, five minutes. Perform that portion of the speech for your imag-inary audience. When you reach the end, *immediately* go back to the beginning of the section and do it again. Be prepared for this, so you don't have to shuffle pages or stop to regroup in any way.

In fact, you should not even try to change your tone or your objective or your action to fit the text you're returning to. Just start it again keeping the spirit you had when you ended it. When you get to the end, go back to the beginning again. Loop the section this way at least three times.

There are several things this will do for you. It will get you in the spirit of *keeping going,* so crucial to the success of any public speaker. It may also help you warm up into the beginning of the section, where you may not have much momentum established.

Try it with another portion of the speech. If it goes well, you may be ready for the more advanced Loop-the-Loop.

Pick another section, or use the same one. Deliver it to your imaginary audience. If you feel you make a particularly strong connection to the text and the audience *at any point,* immediately loop back to the beginning of that section—don't even wait until you get to the end. The idea is to start the piece again with the peak energy of the best part. Keep going, and if something starts to click at any point, loop it back again. You don't always have to go back to the beginning of the passage you've selected for your loop, either: Try looping back to a particular paragraph that you didn't feel very good about. Because you up the level of connection on each loop, it's a great technique for building the energy of communication and bringing the qualities of the strongest parts of the speech to those you experience as the weakest.

Practice both the Loop and the Loop-the-Loop on longer and longer portions of your presentation, eventually looping the entire thing, if it's not too long. (If it's more than half an hour long, looping the whole thing might prove too exhausting.) Refuse to stop and comment or try to fix things, especially in the moment of looping back, where continuity of concentration is key.

The Beats Go On

The Loop Exercise is great for helping you experience the emotional flow from one passage of the speech to the next. But there's also a logical flow to your speech, and now is a good time to make sure you're making the most of it.

Back in chapter 5, you experimented with the idea of "beats," portions of your presentation in which you are playing one particular action vis-à-vis your audience (for example, *cautioning* them about what might happen if unsafe business practices are not addressed, or *titillating* them with exciting results from a new study on consumer buying habits). The logical flow of your presentation has everything to do with how you move from one beat to the next. Take some time now to examine your script or notes and make sure you know how and why you are moving from action to action. If there are paragraphs that you can't associate with a strong action, you need to make some decisions about exactly how you want to use those paragraphs to affect your audience.

Once you think you understand the logical flow of actions and ideas on a passage-by-passage basis, take a step back and see how each of these beats contributes to the persuasive power of your speech as a whole. Looking at the meta-structure of your speech and how you're going to use it should remind you of reasons why you included this stuff in the first place. It will also force you to remember that everything you do and say is for a purpose, and that purpose is all about acting on the audience to achieve a desired result.

KEEPING IT FRESH

The typical Broadway run requires actors to perform the same show eight times a week, a demanding schedule that takes its toll no matter how physically and mentally prepared you are. The primary challenge is to find a way to continue to connect with and enjoy the material, even though you've been down this same road hundreds of times.

If you've been rehearsing your speech hard over a number of days or weeks, you may be experiencing similar difficulties in keeping it alive or exciting for yourself. Your practice sessions may occasionally get boring and tiring, maybe even seem fruitless, since the results of rehearsal are often not immediately evident. Expect these emotional cycles, and try not to let them get you down. Good rehearsing always pays off.

As the day of your speech approaches, you need to make clear choices about how you're going to do certain things, based on what's worked well in your earlier rehearsals. For example, you should have a specific sequence of actions you plan to focus on as you do the speech, and that sequence should be the same every time you do it. If you've been starting the speech from behind the podium and that's been working for you, you should feel free to keep doing it that way. The wild experimentation of the early days has to give way to a process that allows you to get comfortable with the final form of the speech. Keeping certain aspects the same from rehearsal to rehearsal breeds a familiarity that lessens nerves and strengthens your command of the presentation. The trick is to develop a comforting consistency without locking yourself into a debilitating rigidity.

Part of your job as a speaker/actor is to create the illusion that each time you do the speech you're doing it for the first time. As you head into the final stretch, remind yourself that for the audience it *will* be the first time. Take comfort in the fact that the material will be new to them, even if it's old to you.

Keeping it fresh requires continuous attention to what you're trying to achieve. If you lost sight of the larger purposes of your speech as you began to focus on things like identifying key words and developing proper posture, it's time to reinvest in the imaginary audience you've created. Let's say you anticipate about a hundred people in attendance at your presentation. Take a moment to ask yourself: "Of all the people in the world, who would most benefit from hearing my message?" Picture that person and ninety-nine more just like him and you've got your ideal practice audience from here on in. Remember to make their needs the focus of your presentation and your communication is sure to remain lively and purposeful.

Another way to reinvigorate late rehearsals is to experiment with your own state of mind (and body). Feeling stiff? Imagine you've had a couple martinis. (Or however many it takes to loosen you up.) Actually get up and do the speech in an imaginary state of partial inebriation. Activating the imagination in this way is a lot more helpful than yelling at yourself to "Loosen up!"

Of course, the opposite works as well. If you're having trouble getting excited or communicating in an energetic way, imagine downing several cups of coffee before your rehearsal begins and see if it gives you the jump-start you're looking for. (It's *not* a good idea, by the way, to actually imbibe anything potent before performance. Chemically stimulating or dulling your brain can affect you in unexpected and unpleasant ways in a high-stakes performance situation. Best to avoid alcohol altogether and use common sense when it comes to caffeine.)

There are also some simple, concrete things you can do to help you continue to see the speech in new ways. Actor David Garrison, who performed *Titanic* on Broadway more than 650 times, recommends changing some little detail each time to keep it fresh. Put a paper clip or a rubber band in your pocket for one rehearsal, or use a long stick instead of a laser pointer for your slide show. You might find that having some new thing to play with opens up parts of your brain you weren't using before. Along those same lines, try wearing nicer clothes or a little cologne and see what happens. If you *feel* a little different, you may find it affects your performance in positive ways.

Bon Voyeurs

Actor Simon Callow observed that "Rehearsing without the audience is surfing without the waves." What's missing is the thrill of the unknown; the daring encounter with elements you can't control.

That's why the best way to keep your late rehearsals fresh is to add some other live humans into the mix. If you have friends or colleagues who are willing to listen to you, don't hesitate to corral them. It can be a big help to have real human eyes to look into and real human responses to gauge as you speak. Just make sure you know what you want from them before you invite them to listen. Do you want to open yourself up to any criticism they might have? If all you're looking for is bodies in the room who won't talk back afterward, tell them that ahead of time. If you just want to hear compliments to boost your self-confidence, tell them that as well, and make sure you've chosen guinea pigs who will oblige you.

If you want your mock audience to give you a detailed critique of content or delivery, first make sure they're qualified to do so. (Do they know enough about the topic of the speech? The audience? The purpose?) Then give them specific questions to keep in mind to help them focus on what you need to hear. Ask them to pay special attention to your body language or your eye contact or your conclusion, or whatever you think needs work. The most important thing is that you make sure you're ready and able to hear criticism without letting it make you self-conscious or depressed. And be willing to reject any criticism that you disagree with. Smile, nod, and thank them for their time, then continue rehearsing, incorporating as much or as little of their commentary as you see fit.

Vocal Health

If you're not used to doing a lot of speaking, all this rehearsing may be wearing down your voice. Professional actors are notoriously neurotic about vocal health. Which is understandable because, if the voice goes, there's not much you can do but call in the understudy (and risk being replaced for good). As a result, the profession has developed a whole series of rituals and remedies designed to maintain vocal health. And while the demands on you as a speaker may not be quite as rigorous as those on the Broadway performer, you still need to be concerned with the proper care of your voice if you want it to perform admirably on demand.

If you've been concentrating on breathing more efficiently and getting rid of unnecessary tension in your body and throat as you speak, you've gone a long way toward ensuring and sustaining the productivity of your voice.

Even so, you might find yourself occasionally experiencing hoarseness if you're not used to speaking a lot or if you are suffering from a cold. The best remedy for the hoarse voice is vocal rest. Don't talk except when you absolutely need to. And don't whisper— ever. While you might think whispering would protect damaged vocal cords, it actually strains them as much or more than speaking in full voice. You can also combat hoarseness with slippery elm, an organic substance derived from tree bark that is available at most health food stores in the form of lozenges or tea. Any kind of caffeine-free tea, for that matter, mixed with a little honey and lemon, will provide a soothing coat for your throat and allow your natural voice to regain strength.

If you feel a sore throat coming on, the best thing you can do is to gargle. A warm salt water gargle will reduce swelling of the throat and vocal folds, alleviating some of the "thickness" of the sound you are producing. The truly adventurous might want to try an unpleasant tasting sore throat remedy that some actors swear by: gargling with a mixture of two parts warm water to one part apple cider vinegar. Call it brilliant homeopathy or mass hysteria, but many in the acting profession (ourselves included) insist that gargling with this mixture at the first signs of a sore throat not only reduces swelling, but also alleviates pain and staves off more serious throat infections. As with all medical remedies, it's best to check with your doctor if you have any questions or concerns.

The Dress Rehearsal

Actors approach the "final dress" as an exciting opportunity to put all the elements of a production together and begin "living the role" just before opening night. It's a crucial stage of the process, one that gives them the confidence to know they'll be able to deliver the goods at show time. Your rehearsal process should include at least one dress rehearsal the day before your speech. You can do it by yourself or in front of colleagues or friends but, to reap the full benefits, you've got to take it as seriously as you would a performance.

Use a space that approximates as closely as possible the one in which you'll actually be speaking. If you are including visuals in your presentation, make sure you have the proper equipment set up before you begin. Of course, it wouldn't be a dress rehearsal if you didn't do it in costume. Put on whatever clothes you'll be wearing so you get the feel of how to move in those shoes or gesture in that jacket.

Also, imagine that you received whatever introduction you think you might get and start your rehearsal from the moment you take the stage. Practice walking to the podium with confidence and connecting to the audience, then dive into your speech.

Unless you are planning to have an intermission in your presentation, go all the way through the speech without stopping. If you do plan to have a break in the middle, then by all means practice that, too, pausing for the allotted amount of time.

When you've finished your rehearsal, reflect on how it went. You may even want to jot down a few notes about things like your level of confidence, the effectiveness of your body language, how well you presented the logic of your speech, your enthusiasm, your use of visuals—anything you can think of that might be worth evaluating.

Now, before you begin obsessing about the things you want to improve, take a moment to congratulate yourself on what went well. Since the audience isn't there to applaud you yet, you'll have to do it for yourself. After that, you can decide which parts of your delivery you want to continue to work on between now and when you actually give your speech. One cautionary note: Your "needs improving" list will only be useful to you if it is brief, concrete, and manageable. Choose five things that you want to address and focus on those.

As soon as you feel you've made progress in the areas you've identified, do another full run of the speech. Your evaluation this time should concentrate exclusively on what's working for you. When an actor moves into performance mode, he takes ownership of his work and leaves the "woulda, coulda, shouldas" behind. Do the same for yourself. After your final rehearsal, focus all your energy on what's there, not what's not.

Chapter 9

It's Show Time, Folks

"Acting is 95 percent preparation. If you're ready to act, then you can."

—ERIC MORRIS

"PLACES, PLEASE." THESE ARE THE LAST WORDS THE ACtor hears before taking the stage. It's the moment of truth, signaling the end of preparation and the beginning of performance—ready or not, here you come.

And that's how most actors feel right before the curtain rises: both ready and not. Not ready, because after weeks of rehearsal, you're painfully aware of how much there can be to think about (the lines, the blocking, the character's physical and vocal habits), and it's hard not to think about it all. And yet ready, because somewhere deep down you trust that rehearsal has paid off and all that stuff is taken care of. It's become part of your subconscious. The time for worrying about a hundred petty details is over and you must now be in the moment, allowing yourself to respond intuitively and naturally to all the stimuli you experience. It's a truly exhilarating aspect of performing.

FINAL PREPARATIONS

Walk into any theater two hours before the opening-night curtain and you'll be treated to quite a spectacle: actors frantically running through a bit of stage business they couldn't rehearse last night because the paint hadn't dried on the set, technicians scurrying around adjusting and readjusting the lights, prop masters tweaking the placement of vases and suitcases, costume designers fiddling with snarled zippers and unraveled hemlines. And if you look closely enough you'll see one other figure, clipboard in hand, moving calmly about in the eye of the storm. It's the stage manager, the person responsible for making sure the technical cues are set and the actors are focused and ready so the show can go up on time. Stage managers are much beloved figures in the theater because they take charge of the frenetic pre-show environment and allow the performers at least the illusion that everything is under control.

When you deliver your speech, you probably won't have a stage manager to depend on, so you'll have to perform this function for yourself. Following are some tips for taking charge of your speaking environment and getting yourself properly focused as you approach the moment of performance.

The Care and Feeding of You

How you handle yourself throughout the day of your speech can have a big effect on the quality of your performance. The key is to take control of your circumstances at every turn.

Allow yourself plenty of time to get ready before leaving the house or hotel. Warm up, physically and mentally, and take your time getting dressed. Behaving in a calm, relaxed manner will actually make you feel calmer and more relaxed.

It's possible that, in spite of your preparation, you're still experiencing a little nervousness. Remember: That can be a good thing. If you were totally relaxed, you'd be asleep, which probably would not make for a great speech. When your heart is pounding just a bit faster, your brain is getting more blood. You're more alert and actually smarter than usual! Rejoice!

What you eat and drink on the day of your speech also has a lot to do with your ability to perform at your peak. Your preparation ritual should include a balanced, healthy meal. If, like many performers, you suffer from a little nausea when you're nervous, you still need to get something in your stomach to maintain your energy throughout your performance. Eat a big meal several hours before your speech (when you're less likely to experience stomach upset), and then a light snack shortly before showtime.

As your mother probably told you, some foods are better for you than others, and what you eat as a speaker is no exception. In general, you should avoid chocolate and all dairy products shortly before speaking. These foods can produce mucus that coats the vocal cords, creating the need to clear your throat. Also, as we've said before, it's wise to evaluate your tolerance for coffee and other caffeine products on the day of performance. If you're a die-hard coffee drinker, a cup in the morning might be necessary to get your engine started. On the other hand, you'll probably experience an adrenaline boost just before show time and too much caffeine in your system will intensify the pre-show jitters.

Finally, nothing is better for you than water. In fact, doctors recommend you drink eight glasses a day. At the very least, you should make sure you have one lukewarm glass available to drink during your speech.

Props

If you turn to the back of just about any theatrical script, you'll find a property list—a catalog of the physical objects that are vital to the life of the play. *A Midsummer Night's Dream*, for example, calls for love potion, fairy dust, and the head of an ass, among other things. Part of the pre-show ritual for the stage manager is to go through the prop list and make sure everything is where it's supposed to be for the opening curtain. Speakers, too, can gain peace of mind by developing a prop list. Yours probably won't include the head of an ass, but it should contain the following:

A card with the address of the speaking venue and the name and phone number of your primary contact.

Cash for parking and emergencies.

At least two copies of your script, note cards, or outline.

A portfolio or folder for your written materials.

A pen and paper to take notes on other people's presentations and jot down last-minute ideas.

Tissues or a handkerchief.

A glass or bottle of water.

A watch.

Depending on what visuals you're using, you might also need:

Your slides, disks, or transparencies.

A pointer for slides or overheads.

Chalk for blackboards, erasable markers for dry-erase boards, or felt markers for flip charts.

Note: You should also check beforehand to make sure the coordinators of your event are providing the flip chart or whatever projection machinery you need, otherwise you'll need to bring that, too.

The Physical Setup

Most theater schedules demand that the basic elements of the set be completed at least a week before opening night, so the actors can get used to what it feels like to move around in the physical space. Once the actors begin rehearsing on the actual stage, adjustments are often made to accommodate their needs and clear things up for the audience: Furniture gets repositioned for easier access or the blocking gets opened up to provide better sight lines. You never really know how it's all going to work until you've rehearsed several times on the set.

For speakers, however, the process is very different. Often you're asked to perform in public without ever having seen the physical environment in which you'll be speaking. So if you race in moments before giving a presentation—and lots of speakers do—you leave a whole lot up to chance. Is the room configured the way it was supposed to be? Does the microphone work and will it be the right height for you? Can your visuals be seen by the people in the back row? You'd better hope so, because when it's time to speak it's too late to do anything about it.

Once your performance has started it's very easy to get distracted by little things that aren't quite right in the physical environment. Safeguard against this by getting to the space early and checking it out. Pay particular attention to the following:

Podium. Do you want to be in the center or off to the side? Is the height adjustable? Can you comfortably move out from behind it? Is there enough room for your papers and props?

Visual equipment. Is it set up properly? Do you know how to use it? Is someone assisting you and, if so, do they know their cues for changing slides?

Seating arrangement. Is the number of chairs appropriate for the expected size of your audience? Are they close enough to where you're speaking? Are they far enough away? Are the sight lines good from everywhere in the house?

Lighting. Is the level high enough for you and your charts to be seen clearly at the podium? Does it get low enough for maximum visibility of your slides? Do you know how to adjust the lights if necessary?

Sound system. Have you tested the level of your microphone? Do you control the volume or does a technician? Can you adjust its height or move it out of your way if you need to? What position produces the fewest "pops" and other extraneous noises?

Room temperature. If it doesn't feel comfortable to you, it probably won't be for your audience either. Do you know how to control it?

If you can, do a mini run-through of your speech to really get the feel of the place. If something seems not quite right, whether the temperature is too cold or the mike is too "hot," don't be shy about politely expressing your concerns to the event coordinator. Remember that the people responsible for planning the event have the exact same goal you do: to make it the best it can possibly be.

Even if you arrive early, there will sometimes be surprises in the physical setup that you just can't control. If that happens, you've got to be flexible. Do what actors do and improvise. There's an old saying in the theater that "if the roof falls in, let it fall in on your character." Meaning that when you really know who you are and what you're about, you don't need to worry if you get thrown a curve. You'll just handle it, putting on a great front, acting as though that gigantic billboard of a rooster was meant to be there all along.

Waiting in the Wings

When you're speaking as part of a larger program, there are a few additional things you should think about. For one, if you're on a panel or are in any way visible to the audience before your remarks begin, you should be "in character" from the very first moment. Just like an actor who sits silently on stage for ten minutes before delivering his first line, you are part of the play from the opening curtain and should behave in accordance with your role. Everything you do, from laughing at someone's joke to the way you give applause, tells your audience something about you, so make sure you know what you want to say. Being in the role not only helps you create a favorable impression on the audience but also prepares you to be at your best when you step out onto the stage.

Occasionally a speaker who precedes you will inadvertently steal your thunder by making a key point you were going to make or using the same popular reference as an anecdote. If that happens, don't panic. Simply find a way to work the unusual coincidence into your remarks and make a virtue out of it. (After all, great minds think alike, right?) Connecting your remarks to those of the speakers before you is a good idea even if there's no overlapping information. Making connections contextualizes your message for your audience and also demonstrates your ability to be a good listener who understands the big picture.

ALLYING YOURSELF WITH THE AUDIENCE

Many actors like to gauge an audience before they get on stage. As the pre-show sounds drift into the dressing room via the intercom, actors often remark on whether the crowd seems lively and energetic, or quiet and tired. Sometimes even after the show starts, performers who haven't yet made an entrance will gather round to hear how the first real laugh line goes over and use this as a barometer for the level of audience participation they can expect. There's even a whole mythos in the theater about which nights draw the most enthusiastic crowds (Thursdays and Saturdays are traditionally boisterous, Fridays oddly quiet). Obviously there's no exact science here; it's just a way of preparing yourself for what you might encounter when you set foot on the stage.

As a speaker, you may find a little crowd-gauging useful as well. If the presenter before you is a particularly amusing storyteller who, for whatever reason, garners nothing more than a titter here and there, then you can be less discouraged when you receive only a modest response to your first punch line. A less-than-boisterous reception doesn't mean you bombed—the crowd is just quiet, and you've got to let that be okay. In fact, try as you might, you can never really know what they're thinking about your performance. As John Gielgud once wrote, "Last night's audience, which [the actor] cursed for its unresponsiveness, may have enjoyed his performance every whit as much as tonight's, with which he feels the most cordial and personal sympathy."

Audiences, like individuals, have different personalities. So don't jump to the worst conclusions.

No matter what the predisposition of your audience may be, one thing is absolutely certain: You must find a way to make a personal connection with them right off the bat. Calmly approach the podium or microphone and arrange your papers; practice your inward smile; and establish confident, communicative eye contact with several members of the audience before you ever say a word. That's a strong entrance, one that lets your listeners know they're in good hands.

Try to get them actively involved early on in your presentation. If the crowd is small enough, get them to introduce themselves. People want to know who else is in the room. (Of course, if they all know each other already and it's just that *you* want to know who they are, it's better to find out privately before the presentation begins.) You can also involve them by asking a few questions about what their prior experience with your topic has been or what they're hoping to gain from your talk. You can get the same effect with a larger audience by conducting a "show of hands" poll relevant to your subject matter (for example, "How many of you have ever visited a prison?").

Find out why they're there, what they want from you. As you deliver your speech, you should feel free to insert an occasional comment that points out how you're addressing the concerns they've stated. Knowing a little about your audience breaks down barriers and gives you a chance to direct specific parts of your speech to particular people. ("As a longtime advocate for prison reform, Ms. Jones probably has some first-hand knowledge of this . . ."). Even if your speech is prepared word for word, you can use the information they've given you to help you decide with whom to make eye contact or where to place your vocal emphasis.

Allying yourself with the audience means creating a positive relationship, even if your message may be hard for them to swallow. As you're well aware, you have an objective, something you want the audience to do. But sometimes getting what you want involves giving them what they want. That's why it's important to be aware of their needs and to do your best to identify with them. Too often speakers consciously or unconsciously cast the audience as the enemy. Pursuing an objective doesn't have to be a matter of head-to-head conflict in which there can be only one winner.

As you deliver the speech, try to keep a win–win attitude. No matter how difficult your message is for them to hear, do everything you can to help them understand how what you want is at least as valuable to them as it is to you. Which is just another way of saying: *Speak for your listeners' benefit, not your own.* It's the golden rule of public speaking, and the secret formula for success.

Distracted Audiences

The hero begins a slow, brave walk to the gallows. Suddenly he stops, turning his searing gaze on his executioners. As he opens his mouth to utter his triumphant last words, the jarring snap, crackle, and pop of a candy wrapper rattles through the audience. The spell is broken.

Or is it?

Actors know that there will always be people for whom there's no time like the present to enjoy a handful of Skittles. That's why you can't let yourself get unnerved by every minor distraction in the house, and you certainly can't take it personally. Seasoned performers salvage dramatic moments in the face of little disturbances all the time, simply by making what they're doing more interesting than what's going on in the audience. Instead of allowing themselves to be distracted, they recommit with even more energy to the actions they are playing, all but daring anyone to look away.

This strategy can be equally effective for public speakers, but it is too often underutilized. Many inexperienced speakers get derailed by the lone yawner or the guy in the back who just can't seem to get his Palm Pilot under control, and they lose sight of their speaking objectives. It's important to keep in mind that there are all kinds of reasons why someone in the crowd might not be giving you their full attention, most of which have nothing to do with you. They may have been up half the night with a crying baby or maybe they're obsessing over a hangnail. You simply can't know.

If most people in your audience appear to be involved in your presentation, then your best strategy is to ignore the isolated offender and keep doing what you're doing. If, on the other hand, doodling and paper shuffling are the dominant trends among your listeners, you need to shake things up. These and certain other behaviors you may notice—like drooping eyelids, coughing, staring out the window, fidgeting, and squirming—are telltale signs that you're losing them. A good response would be to vary your pitch or tempo, change your position in the room, ask an impromptu question, or remind them where your talk is headed (what the payoff will be and why the information at hand is important to it). If the situation seems really serious, you might even invite them to stand up and stretch for a moment. Bad responses include apologizing, giving up, blaming yourself and your lack of talent, and blaming the audience and taking it out on them.

Sometimes you'll pick up on something that goes beyond a mere lack of interest—the crowd is not so much bored as hostile to your point of view. When an audience turns on you, it's usually for one of the following reasons:

They don't understand your message.

They don't see the relevance of your message to their situation.

They have preconceived notions that make them disbelieve your message.

They see your message as a potential threat to their well-being and therefore reject it.

Any one of these scenarios can make a listener lose interest or, worse, become downright antagonistic. So now let's take a look at how to handle a presentation that is getting a negative response.

The Madding Crowd

Hooks, catcalls, boos, gongs, rotten tomatoes, scathing reviews. . . . Over the centuries, theatergoers have developed some pretty inventive ways of expressing dissatisfaction with performers and performances. In the civilized world (the world outside of theater, that is), people can generally be counted on to behave with a greater sense of decorum, but hostile audiences are still an occasional force for the speaker to reckon with. If people in your audience are resisting your message—raising objections, voicing criticism, or otherwise exhibiting the outward signs of disapproval—there are several things you can do to bridge the divide. The first, and perhaps most important, is to disengage your ego so that you can listen objectively and really try to understand their concerns. Once you understand where the opposition is coming from, it's much easier to deal with.

If there's a genuine difference of opinion—you think the neighborhood library should include a community recreation room and they think the building should be used for reading only—give them an opportunity to voice their objections and "get on the scoreboard." If you probe to find out why they're so resistant to your idea, you might hear something like this: They're worried a recreation room would draw in too many young people from the neighborhood, creating a rambunctious atmosphere that would disrupt the routine of regular library users.

Instead of getting your hackles up and immediately defending your position, try first to acknowledge that their concern is a reasonable one. (If you really try, you can find *some* merit in almost every objection). Nine times out of ten, all it takes to defuse hostility is a little sensitivity. "I think you raise a very important point. We need to find a way to provide a safe place for young people to meet at the library while preserving the quiet atmosphere that so many of us go there to enjoy. Let's take a few minutes to talk about how that might work."

By giving their position some credibility, you no longer cast yourself as the enemy and you can begin to work in partnership with them to solve the problem.

No matter how much opposition you receive from your audience, you'll always do better to treat them like partners rather than adversaries. Keep your composure, remain respectful, listen without interrupting. If you really feel at a loss, try verbally mirroring what you are hearing from them. "If I understand correctly, many of you are afraid that the essential character of the library will change if we add this room." Reflective listening (a technique employed by mediators, therapists, and other professionals whose job it is to facilitate constructive dialogue) is a great way to let people know that you've understood them and that you care about the issues they raise. It also buys you some valuable time to find a way to gently get the discussion back on course.

Once you've built a bridge between you and the oppositional audience, it's time to move on. The speaker who tries to address every possible objection runs the risk of losing control of his speech altogether. Try getting back on track by reminding them where the speech is headed and letting them know how they can continue to follow up with you if they're not yet satisfied. "I appreciate your input and will certainly share your concerns with the planning committee. What I'd like to do now is to continue describing the plans we've designed so far, then I'll stop and take more questions and comments."

THE Ps & Qs OF Q & A

The question-and-answer period provides a unique opportunity to connect with the audience and respond directly to their needs and concerns. It is not only an effective forum for exchanging ideas but also a powerful means of clearing up misunderstandings and effecting change in the minds of your listeners.

Try to make a virtue out of every question, as if you'd been hoping someone would pipe up and ask this very thing. In so doing you'll not only invite meaningful dialogue but also project a much-needed sense of confidence in the positions you are representing. Even the most controversial and hostile questions can ultimately help you. At least now the objections are out in the open and you can counter them. By asking a question, an audience member is giving you a chance to change his mind rather than simply shutting down. You can now work to promote mutually beneficial dialogue.

An easy way to foster a positive relationship with an audience during the Q & A is to preface responses with brief affirmative (but truthful) statements like "I appreciate your question"—which you should, since it gives you another opportunity to make your point—or "I know that's a concern for all of us." Affirming the validity of the questions also encourages shy people and those suffering from stage fright to feel comfortable jumping into the discussion. Avoid "That's a good question," however. It can come off as condescending, because the questioner probably assumed the question was good (or she wouldn't have asked it).

Structuring Q & A

Whether your audience is openly hostile or wildly sympathetic to your cause, getting them to participate productively in question-and-answer sessions requires a little finesse. Your job is to guide the audience through the participation process, letting them know what's expected of them and what they can expect of you. Make sure it's clear from the beginning of the presentation how you'll handle questions—will the audience be encouraged to ask them throughout, during periodic pauses, or only at the end? Different presentations benefit from different Q & A structures. If you're walking through the details of a difficult procedure, you may want to take questions throughout, to ensure that your listeners under-stand each complicated step. If you're giving a fun talk on hot va-cation spots, you might want to ask people to save their questions until the end. The big advantage of taking questions only after you're done talking is that you won't have to address issues out of sequence or risk running out of time before you get to your most important points.

The opportunity to exchange ideas with the speaker is one of the most valuable aspects of most public speaking situations. Once they've participated in a dialogue, audience members are far more likely to retain and act on what they've heard. If you find, therefore, that you won't have time for a formal Q & A, you should offer to stick around after the speech is over to answer questions.

Mum's the Word

One of the hardest things for a speaker to do is to engage a quiet audience. If you want to promote a lively exchange, you've got to frame the discussion in lively terms. Asking "Are there any ques-tions" suggests the possibility that there aren't, which means the audience might get to go to lunch early. Surprise—no questions today! "Is that clear?" is also a weak opening, because it implies that you're not sure of your ability to explain things well or you think the audience isn't quite smart enough to get it.

In general, avoid yes or no questions. "What concerns do you have that we haven't specifically addressed yet?" will probably yield a richer response than "Is there anything else you'd like to know?"

If you have reason to believe the Q & A might be really sluggish, you might want to prepare a stimulating question or two to start things off. ("When I speak around the country, I'm often asked . . .") Once you get the ball rolling, people will be much more likely to pick it up and run with it.

Directing the Dialogue

Once the questions start coming, *listen to them.* Make sure you really understand what the questioner is getting at before you dive into an answer. If you're uncertain, probe more deeply into the question or ask a follow-up. Find out what they really want to know so you can frame an answer that will hit home. Your listeners will appreciate the extra effort.

If someone asks you a real stumper, don't be afraid to admit you don't know the answer. It's perfectly appropriate to suggest a resource where the answer can be found or to offer to find out that information yourself and get back to them. Or, if you're speaking to people who might have expertise in the subject, open the question up to the audience and see if anyone else has a suggestion. Whatever you do, don't try to guess or bluff your way through an answer. Contrary to popular belief, speakers actually rise in the audience's esteem when they honestly admit they don't know. No one has all the answers, so why should you?

If someone asks something entirely off-topic, you should politely decline to answer it. Let the questioner know that you don't have the time to get into that now since your presentation was specifically about *x*, but you'd be happy to discuss it with him afterward.

On a related note, beware of creating a situation in which a small number of people dominate the entire question-and-answer session. You control who gets to ask the questions, so include as many people as you can. Keep your responses brief and to the point so you'll have time to answer as many questions as possible. Also, don't forget that even when you're addressing a particular questioner, you still need to speak for the benefit of all your listeners. Continue to make eye contact with the group as you answer each question, to avoid turning your public speech into a private conversation.

Keep track of the time and let your audience know when you'll be taking only a couple more questions. Always try to end your Q & A session on a high note, taking as your final question one that you can really bat out of the ballpark. Then thank your audience for their participation and wrap it up.

APPLAUSE, APPLAUSE

The curtain call is the audience's chance to thank the performer for work well done. It's an important part of the overall communication and one that should not be rushed. If the bows seem perfunctory, the audience feels cheated.

Although a public speaker shouldn't actually take a bow, the principle is the same. End your speech clearly and stick around to graciously accept applause before you leave the stage. As soon as the applause reaches its peak, you can begin your exit. And, by all means, get off the stage before the clapping stops altogether.

Knowing how to accept compliments after the show is also part of your work as a speaker. If someone says they liked your speech, the appropriate response is "Thank you," not, "Well, it wasn't much, really" or, heaven forbid, "Actually I was better in rehearsal." Self-effacing comments like these suggest false modesty at best, extreme neurosis at worst. They also insult the compliment giver by implying that she doesn't know a good speech from a bad one.

THE REVIEWS ARE IN

What do you do after it's all over? Well, for one, we hope you'll go out for a relaxing meal or back to your hotel for a bubble bath. You deserve a reward for all the hard work you've done.

Once you've gotten a little distance from the speaking event, you can start to reflect on how it went. Every performance is like a dress rehearsal for the next time you have to do it, so the more you understand about how it affected your audience, the better off you'll be.

Some actors—Katherine Hepburn, Stockard Channing, and Anthony Hopkins among them—never read their reviews while they're in the run of a show. They know they can't make radical changes in their performance once the play has officially opened, and they don't want to start second-guessing themselves based on one critic's opinion.

Speakers, however, usually have more latitude when it comes to shaping their speeches for future performances. By reading the evaluations from your audience or eliciting verbal feedback, you'll get a feel for what connected with them, what didn't, and why. If you find that they liked your style, but thought your content was weak, then you should go back to the writing phase of your speech development process. If they seemed to get the substance but were not wowed by the delivery, reexamine your verbal and physical communication choices.

You also need to have a little perspective when you read your reviews. Most of us are far more likely to remember one harsh comment than forty raves, which is a shame. When you make big changes based on a lone voice of dissent, you cheat future audiences out of all the good stuff that's already working for you. Your sense of how it went when you were up at the podium is every bit as important as what people are writing in their evaluations. So, as with everything else having to do with public speaking, to thine own self be true. Learn what you can from the constructive criticism, work to hone your message and your style, but never sacrifice your basic confidence in yourself as someone worthy of holding center stage.

Index